Copyright © Charles O'Boyle, 2020
All Rights Reserved Worldwide

Table of Contents   **Page**

Dedication ii

Prologue iii

1. Beware of the Ides of March! 1
2. USA Historic Diary: Hell Weeks, March 9-16, 2020 8
3. Panics: Causes & Effects 18
4. Five W's: Who, When, What, Where, Why & How! 31
5. Business, Industry & Government Impact 42
6. Global: Social/Economic/Political & Legal Shock 49
7. TRUMP's Wall Street Rally 2016 – 2020 62
8. USA "Make America Rich Again" Dream? 69
9. MAGANOMICS: C+I+G: Boom or Bust? 75
10. Past & Present World Panics! 81
11. POTUS Daily Briefings: Washington, DC 86
12. Don't Just Stand There: Do Something! 104
13. Broken/Antiquated FED GOV Systems 109
14. USA! USA!...Nobody Bats Zero! 119
15. ERISA: 1980s to 2020 (Your 401Ks!) 124
16. Future Panics: N.B.C & Cyberspace! 130
17. Lessons Learned: After the Panics! 135

Epilogue 144

Bibliography 146

Appendix A: Future 2020 Security 148

Dedication

I dedicate the writing of this book, to my fellow alumni at both Northeastern University in Boston, Massachusetts and to Babson College in Wellesley, Massachusetts, among whom, I am honored to have graduated with Honors, while attending both schools on the Post WWII GI Bill!

Charles V. O'Boyle, Sr. AS, BS Northeastern University, Boston, MA; MBA Babson College, Wellesley, MA.

"To strive, too seek, to find, not to yield!" , from Homers Odyssey, 675-725 BC!

Prologue

Throughout this Planet Earth's long history, mankind has been in turmoil; whether it has been in wars with its population, neighbors, foreigners or with its precious, originally, unspoiled Mother Nature. However, not until the 20th Century has man recognized, through his destructive powers, the meager, fragile existence that surrounds our very survival.

As we ponder our present-day modern existence with all our comfort factors in place, one would think that we can deal with any problem immediately, with precise solutions. Our superb USA culture, training, schooling, and winning track record illustrates many grand examples of such endeavors. From winning World Wars to landing on the Moon!

In our first Quarter of the 21st century, we seem to have become invincible after overcoming wars, old diseases, ailments, maladies, even Space. Just when we have about achieved a high-level, "Nirvana State" tragedy strikes! Enemies are suddenly all around us, whether it be visible or invisible!

<u>ATTENTION…!</u> Everybody! We are having an epidemic, perhaps even a pandemic…now everyone panics!

This is what is happening in the timeframe of March 2020, all over the Planet Earth, people are in a panic state! What to do about this new, unseen invisible force? What to do is on everyone's mind. Our comfort factors are being attacked at a furious rate never seen in modern history! Such chaos, occurring even in the so-called enlightened population place we call home, the United States of America!

How did it happen: Another 911.2! Another Pearl Harbor 1941.2? Another crash and depression of 1929.2? Who is responsible? Where, again, was our protection? Where were our many interdiction systems in place to prevent or mitigate and quickly end this kind of World chaos?

Living in the most powerful nation on the planet, the USA, with every possible convenience and protection up to and including our walled and guarded gated bedroom communities, somewhere, somehow, out of the blue, an archaic unknown enemy is disturbing our very existence.

I am writing this on March 19, 2020, several days into the abyss. What is happening is beyond our imagination, beyond are in-place controls and Early Warning Systems of the Cold War 1960s, both government, military, economic and financial.

How long will it last? Is on everyone's mind. How can it be fixed? Who was responsible? Can someone connect the dots? These are questions that go unanswered as of this March, April, May 2020 dates.

Our Fed Gov leaders, every day, appear on our new 55-inch or greater, state-of-the-art, 5G high-definition TVs. The expression on their faces does not show confidence. We, again, the USA, are not ready for such an unknown attack.

One's mind wonders to similar events that have occurred in our lifetime or in our history books. The Plague that occurred worldwide in the year 1918, the attack on Pearl Harbor 1941 and who can forget 911! We will try to answer some of the questions that were just posed. We will delve into the mysteries of epidemics and pandemics of the 20th century. We need and deserve answers now!

We will compare our 250 year old Federal Systems and new 20 & 21st High-Tech Industry and even NASA mission success tools and controls that, in hind sight, had they been in force, could have prevented what might be a "bet the farm" event, never before dealt with in our so-called over-controlled free-world country!

Hopefully, after reading this book, what will result, are recommended corrective and preventative actions that will be immediately implemented to preserve, protect, and defend our USA way of life!

These critical lessons-learned and systemic fixes are designed to close significant panic and failure gaps that exist in our present government, economic and financial systems.

1. Beware of the Ides of March!

"The day the 2020 market died!" Op-ed

On March 15, 44 BC, Julius Caesar, Roman General & Statesman was assassinated by conspiring Senators, notable was a name called Marcus Brutus! Caesar's rule and murder ended the Roman Empire! "Et tu. Bruti"! Caesar remarks, in one of Shakespeare's famous tragedy!

Stocks fall in another day of market turmoil, erasing the "Trump Bump."

Photo 1.0 Wall Street traders faced with a never-before panic and crash of March 2020! (NY Times photo)

March, throughout history has always been a capricious timeframe from the time of the Caesars of the Holy Roman Empire. On my first trip to Rome landing at the Leonardo De Vinci Airport and passing by a big Roman Empire Map on large, highway bill-board sign. I felt that I too was returning to my native roots at least half of them…Italian.

Italy loves the tourist, especially Americans with their search for the finest places and cultural classics that are certainly offered here in huge quantities…whether it be the gastronomical delights from cappuccino to native wine or to classic pasta dishes and after meal gelato with Sambuca on the side! All offerings tantalize every one of our human senses to extreme measures, searching for the absolute best of everything consumed.

In many trips to Italy, one of my most favorite places on the Planet, I noticed the continuous inflow of Asians, first in a tourist role, then in worker situations. Since my first trip in 1990, I noticed tour buses of Asians, just like me an American, seeking to take in all the historical sites. Whether it be the Colosseum in Rome or Uffizi Gallery in Florence or marvelous canals of Venice.

This could explain why Italy was hit so hard by the 2020 COVID-19 invader. For it is the best Chinese tradition to return to their native country homes to be with families at the Chinese New Year in January! This may have added to the World's dilemma of the virus spread so quickly in Italy, even over the globe!

My Chinese connection began while just changing Manager jobs and moving from my beloved Route 128 Boston arena to the home of the then Baltimore Colts/DC Beltway! It was back to the big leagues for me, the Martin Company now called Martin Marietta.

I landed there in 1983! The place was Middle River Maryland, close to the downtown area of Baltimore City.

As a newly hired manager, new kid on the block, I was chosen to be given a special assignment!

For the next several workdays, I was to be the company's escort for the then first Chinese trade delegation on its Baltimore-Washington tour of facilities throughout the region.

Perhaps it was my good first impression with top management that Martin picked me. Or perhaps I was the only manager who was not totally engaged that led me to such an opportunity. I was introduced to the 12 or more Chinese country representatives, all dressed in their Chairman Mao military uniforms, the group was made up of both male and female members.

Later, I was told that they bought one of everything that they saw! After work, each day and at lunchtime, we were taken to the highest-class Asian restaurants in the DC area for closed-door eating and drinking sessions. We were the only customers there and were given top-shelf, red-carpet treatment.

Upon introduction we exchanged business cards. Mine was printed only in English. Theirs were in English on one side and Chinese on the other. I still have those cards as souvenirs! Their titles were as high as one can go in government. Mostly identified as Procurement Directors for the entire country of China. People who bought all the military products along with their Management Assistants.

All were on their best behavior. Most of the males chain-smoked in our social settings, such as long lunches and evening dinners.

I stopped smoking after leaving the U.S. Army years ago.

Perhaps the only reason that I smoked was to earn a break from the long marches and to take what the NCOs called a "smoke break". Everyone participated, we all lit up! Later, we did cigarette butt checks of the grounds making sure that no evidence existed of our presence. You were even offered free WWII rations such as Old Golds and Raleigh cigarettes brands that were not even sold any more.

I was always curious as to what the females in the group did. Although I noticed them writing down almost every conversation that was heard or they were exposed to. It was difficult to determine if any of them spoke English or understood English, since few spoke a word.

Later, I was told that the leaders right-hand, was a female officer who had a PhD, with Honors, from MIT in Electrical Engineering! MIT was a short distance from my undergraduate school, Northeastern University in Boston!

Surprise, these people were all experts in the field of high-technology! Recall this was in the year of 1983 almost 40 years ago. Even when I worked at NASA, my Systems Engineering Managers were China born MIT Graduates!

"Think about the unthinkable"….the Babson College MBA Course is entitled, Creative Decision-Making, whose Professor remarked during a Group Brainstorming assignment. OK readers let us put that student's hat on! The mind wonders leading to, outside the box, scenarios…unexplored regions to new thinking results!

For me, using my somewhat over-educated mindset, this flashback hit me hard in March 2020, while watching the 2017 Michael Douglas thriller movie entitled, **"Unlocked"!**

The movie involved an "unthinkable" scenario, a biological agent carefully placed in several glass-enclosed, over-crowded International Mall elevators, that when released, was designed to cause a World-wide pandemic, apocalyptic event! I will not spoil the ending for you who have not seen it!

Does Hollywood reflect real-life or is real-life reflected in the movies? Or both? This book's, you are now reading, catch title hit me as I was watching daily national and world events unfolding on a long winter's day in March 2020 at my snowbird residence in the Sunshine State of Florida.

Wow! I told my wife, the Panic of 2020, happening right before our very eyes! World History is now being made! What a great book title, I said…and that is how it all began!!! My fourth published book of 2020! **_"The $Panic of 2020!_**

What is it? It is not a toothache. It is not a headache. It is not like physical pain of any type. It is like death itself, perhaps we are all thinking about a Depression 2.0? I sensed the future pain, the future anguish, the future poverty, the future failures! However, will it last one 2020 calendar quarter, the next week, perhaps even 6-18 months or more? Take your pick, like a multiple-choice quiz! Your guess and mine is as good as theirs!

A colossal event is happening right before our eyes on the biggest video screens mankind has ever produced, with such a high-quality picture as to appear three-dimensional! So hard to watch, day after day. Day one, day two, three for a 5, 6, 7, 8 etc. etc.! Who can stop it? Is there anyone on the planet who can help…anybody! Calling 911! Any team, any light to be seen through what seems like a long-endless hazardous tunnel of nothing but additional anguish, torture, and pain.

So, we begin again, and not since, over 10 years ago, on 911 has the US of A begin to feel such suffering.

"Give me your tired, your poor, your wretched refuse yearning to breathe free, send them, the homeless tempest tossed to me, let them rest upon my golden shores." Statue of Liberty, NYC Harbor.

Our forefathers passed through these NYC gates to America years ago. They brought with them aspirations of hope for a new life. Generations later, we have achieved that goal and more. Our off-spring now enjoy the fruits of our and their labor. Do not underestimate the depth and length of these sacrifices. War after War, turmoil after turmoil, disappointment after disappointment, we have seen many periods of both the agony and the ecstasy. But this time it is different. Our systems in place dealt with the problems before, whether it be tornadoes, hurricanes, or mild epidemics. But, never a full-blown pandemic. Not in modern times.

In preparation for writing this 2020 book. I searched the web for movies on the subject. We already discussed one, **_"Unlocked"_**!

One other was the 1995 Thriller entitled **_"Outbreak"_** with Dustin Hoffman and every male's favorite actress from the redo of **_"The Thomas Crown Affair"_**, Rene Russo! This one, mentioned earlier, was one I missed back then and provides great entertainment by superb cast.

And another Hollywood virus movie is with Matt Damon entitled, ***"Contagion"*** that deals with the 2002-4 SARS and 2009 Pandemic FLU!

For you 2020 generation fans, the Korean movie ***"FLU"*** is also well done, tracing the then, Avian Flu to its maximum damage level. Even USA intervention is shown at the end of a scary video time. The little Korean girl actress deserves an Academy Award for her real-life performance. I hope you get a chance to watch it!

Back to the task at hand interesting reader! Let us Panic of 2020, March onward!

2. USA Historic Diary: Hell Weeks, March 9-16, 2020

"These are the times that try men's souls!"
Thomas Paine, <u>The Crises</u>, December 23, 1776

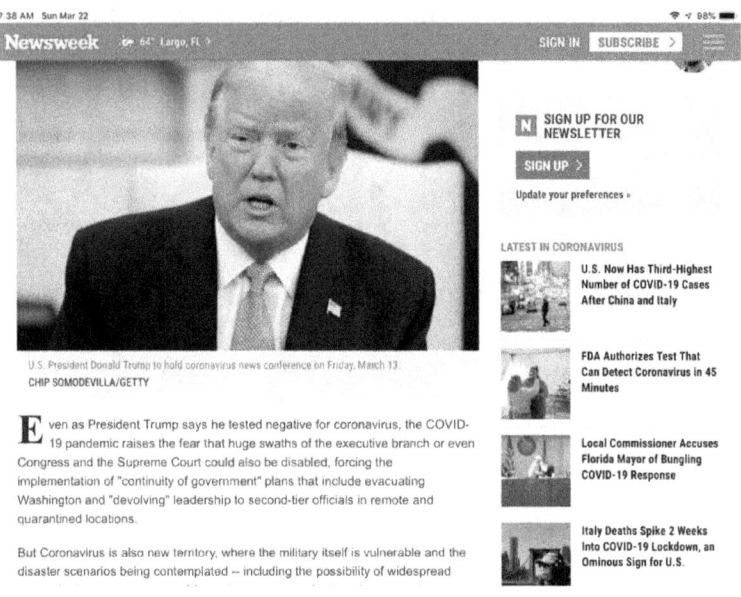

Photo 2.1 Newsweek web-site photo of POTUS addressing nation on TV daily during event!

This photo above is what appeared day after day on every TV station on the planet! I watched it daily as the POTUS addressed, as best he could, under the unknown circumstances, actions he and his Crises Team of "Experts" were taking to deal with what he termed "an unknown invisible enemy" attacking, unabated, the USA!

The last chance to get out of the financial markets, in my judgement, was Valentine's Day, February 15, 2020!…it's over, a Sweetheart Boom of the last 10 years or was it 12!

For me, the ideal time was August 24, 2018! Look at the Daily trading volume…a record day for those close to the vest, Wall Street players. Over the past two years, we 401K folks have not recovered since that day! In fact, since the 2008 Housing Market collapse our 401Ks have not yet fully recovered our losses or as they say, "paper money gains"!

But back to today, Calendar day, Thursday, March 19, 2020! **Stop the bleeding!** I kept thinking as I watched for days now, starting from a Wall Street DOW level of 30,000 high and falling nearly 10,000 points with little or no control or Fed Gov oversight . Sure, there were the so-called circuit breakers from 2008 crash years ago, designed and set to kick in service at 7%, 12%, and 20% drops... and they did… and were executed over and over, hopelessly, for days.

Let us now however, step back and use an analogy from medical technology practice. The patient comes into the HOSPITAL Emergency Room (ER) bleeding profusely as I was after a serious car accident many years ago. After hitting a telephone poll with a new driver, and with no safety belt, I catapulted into the windshield…taking out the rear-view mirror on the way! What to do? I was asked, as I walked into the Emergency Room of the local and only hospital. Who is your Doctor? What if I was unconscious? "Doctor Walsh", I replied, who eventually showed up nearly an hour later and yelled, "doesn't anyone here know how to stop the bleeding?"

For a head wound, it was to apply force to several pressure points which he immediately demonstrated, while I was bleeding to death, to the amazed hospital ER staff of helpless onlookers. Thank You, Dr. Walsh for saving my life!

So, in Wall Street's March 2020's case, what was needed for someone to apply pressure point action to save the patient more importantly, in this case… The US economy from collapse!

Where are the "disconnects" as we used to say at NASA, in conducting engineering analysis of any potential systemic failure. As Harry Truman's Oval office sign read *"The Buck Stops Here"!* And Ronald Reagan's famous POTUS sign, that read, *"I Know, It Can Be Done!* One that I bought at his Semi Valley, CA Presidential Library!

Specifically, let us look at the USA Fed Gov System, and it is focus on the 535 select few in DC, representing the 328,239,523 (2017 Pop.) truly trivial many of us! This was so aptly described by the Italian Economist Pareto in his treatise called Pareto's 80/20 Rules. Our so-called career politicians, some of whom are approaching their 80th year with the average age of 50 in the House and 70 in the Senate.

Most of whom, perhaps even the POTUS, are at on the other side of the digital divide, since only a few attended schools such as mine at Babson College in the 1970s that used computers and in every MBA Class taught. We had two systems in a brand-new computer facility with many terminals, one from HP and the other a DEC Vax Networked System!

Looking closely at this chosen few, elected by the people, a privileged few, who they are and how they got there and what is their net worth is. As Harry Truman once said, "show me a rich politician and I'll show you a crook!" A retired POTUS, Harry retired on his WWI Officers pension and later, a charitable Congress awarded him a few extra dollars to help him survive. He even drove his car back to Missouri as he exited the highest level in the Nation's office! Probably bought the gas too…give them hell Harry!

Our USA House of Representatives, 435 members from 50 states. These are the so-called Baby Boomers, following us, the Silent Generation and a few members preceding called Generation X! Specifically, my off-spring and a younger new generation. Most of whom are part of the chosen profession called lawyers. I know them, my Son, JR is a NY Bar member! And a lot of them come from the Ivy League schools, so-called in old times, as Philadelphia Lawyers….quite a status at that time!

As an engineering career manager, we always looked at lawyers and doctors as practicing professionals. I do not recall ever calling engineering as a practice. Our mistakes here cause significant loss of life and so many litigation actions. For example, look at the Boeing 737Max debacle? I could write a book on that fiasco with cost going on over $10 Billion and climbing! And just the other day, a $60 Billion Fed Gov bail out was requested, after almost spending billions in payouts for just two deadly accidents.

Our USA Senate, a prestigious group of distinguished Americans. Not an easy seat to win for the weak at heart. 100 of the best of the best politicians on the earth, who can easily walk and chew gum at the same time, while giving one the feeling of meeting a high-level religious leader and renown physician at the same time.

Again, a law degree from an Ivy League school helps one get here and a recognizable, down through the ages name, with fame, helps one climb this ladder to a set for life level (SFL). There are no blue-collar folks in this elite club!

It is extremely hard to find anyone in DC who is not, from average American status, is not rich. Some are extraordinarily rich, a few are filthy rich as we call many retirees here in the Sunshine state.

Recessions seldom effect their life-styles...as we used to say a recession is when your neighbor is out of work, a depression is when you are out of work! For that matter, perhaps neither will a depression affect their life-styles! The old story of the rich Philadelphia family comes to mind, who needed to reduce their mansion staff during the 1929 Depression! I think that best describes the impact on the DC folks!

As a retired winning government proposal writer, especially for the Oak Ridge National Laboratory's contract in the 1980s. For which I received a nice Award by the Vice-President, who led the project. Let us review that effort.

At the time, Oak Ridge had many Ph.D.'s in Nuclear Science working there. Today, 40 years later there are 4500 there, 1000 less than 2010, with a $4.6B Budget according to Science Magazine!

How many ways can we split the atom?

Compare this to the Center for Disease Control (CDC) in Atlanta at its approximate 10,899 employees. And a Budget of $6.6B with many MDs/Ph.Ds., who honor the staff at that location.

In 2020, it seems that we are no more prepared today for a biological warfare threat than we were 40 years ago! It may be even less perhaps today, with more threatening planet enemies, I would argue.

Look at our USA DOD, a defense's superior in every military branch. US Army (my pleasure to serve), US Navy (best Top Guns pilots on the planet!), Marines (God bless them all), Air Force (love those pilots too!) and Coast Guard (keep us safe) and now the Space Force (Thanks POTUS Trump!).

And remember those 17 Government agencies mentioned again and again in those long POTUS Trump court-like TV trails and costly (in more ways than just dollars….do the COVID-19 timeline) impeachment hearings. The Agencies given complete knowledge of the others by the former administration, but still not being able to connect the dots in a timely manner!

Next question…what about COVID-19 or 20 or 21? Where is the responsibility for this new invisible enemy? Is it the Army, Navy, Marines, Coast Guard, Space Force? How about the CIA, FBI, NSA, or IRS surely there are thousands of personnel around the globe and in DC? And what about the popular handoff of the difficult tasks, the many Beltway Contractors…too numerous to mention here!

As President Eisenhower repeatedly warned of the military/Industrial complex during the later years of his administration! IKE forecasted that the military-industrial complex would eventually be in charge. We have the best Army, Navy, Marines and Coast Guard defenders and now the Space Force, finest on the planet! So where are our weak spots?

Just look at the many James Bond movie subjects of the past 50 years or is it 55 years, unthinkable enemies list every feature. Our military academies at West Point, Annapolis, Colorado Springs are second to none, just visit them as I have! Amazing places, and I said in my earlier book on MBAs, the Army's West Point Military Academy even offers a course on how to think, profound!

What we will cover next is a series of those involved at the Fed Gov level in dealing with this panic of 2020. They, once identified for your reading pleasure, might seem like an alphabet soup of names, however, are made up of many hard-working servants…called civil servants…who spend their entire careers in government service.

First one called The New Department of Homeland Security (DHS), a cabinet level department started after our 911 attack! 220,000 employees here, Budget $76,000,000,000 in 2021 (down by $12.5B from 2020)! Charter: Keep USA Safe! Against terrorism and other hazards!

Following another Cabinet level Agency, The Department of Health and Human Services (HHS). Employees: 80,000; Budget: $1.3T, yes trillion, plus $94.5B for discretionary authority! Charter: Oversees key Public Health Offices & Programs & Advisory Committees!

National Institute of Health (NIH) – Employees 18,646, Budget: $41.7B. Charter: Biomedical and Scientific Research! (www.healthcare.gov)

And the Department of Defense (DOD) - Budget $718B, Personnel: 2,870,000. Charter: National Security!

Next: Federal Emergency Management Agency (FEMA) – 11,300 employees, Budget $29B. Charter: Help people before and after disasters!

Moving on to the Center of Disease Control & Prevention (CDC) – 15,000 employees, Budget $6.6B. Charter: Rapid & reliable response to Congress requests for information, briefings. Technical Assistance on public health policy & legislative issues!

And now, the Federal Drug Administration (FDA) - 17,388 employees, Budget $6.2B. Charter: Ensure safe and effective drugs for human use!

The Securities and Exchange Commission (SEC) - Personnel: 4,694, Budget: $1.46B. Charter: Protect Investors, Maintain Orderly & Fair Markets, Facilitate Capital Formation!

The Federal Reserve System (FRS) – Employees: 19,433, Budget: $1.225 Billion! Charter – Regulating Banking System (12 Fed Branches in US), Maximizing Employment, Moderating Interest Rates!

Lastly for now, the Federal Deposit Insurance Corporation (FDIC), Budget $2B , 5,755 employees. Charter – provides insurance for depositors of Banks & Credit Unions.

Not to end yet! The Center for Biological Evaluation & Research (CBER) here! Regulates biological products for human use under federal laws.

Do you want me to stop now? Yes, I will!

But the big one you are looking for, not USA, but UN Agency, entitled the W.H.O. (World Health Organization)!

W.H.O. has 7,000 personnel, with a $4.422 Billion budget in 194 member states.

Photo 2.2 W.H.O. Headquarters in Geneva, Switzerland. (NY Times Photo)

The USA traditionally contributes between $100 - $114 Million per year, however, in 2017, it was given $401M that's ($401,000,000)! By 2018-9 US gave $800 Million!

Focus in now on this UN Agency W.H.O. W.H.O's charter is to protect all of us, the entire planet!

Investigations are now underway to determine if perhaps shortcomings of this mission that may have caused the pandemic of 2020. We will need to see as time passes.

Latest news on 4/15/2020. from the Joint Chiefs of Staff Office is that investigations are now underway to determine the Chinese Wuhan Laboratory involvement of the origin of the COVID-19 Virus! Again, time will tell how this turns out! That certainly will be covered in Part II of this book!

Photo 2.3 Wuhan, China National Biosecurity Laboratory (archieve.is photo)

So, now, do you have any idea who is responsible for the COVID-19 Pandemic of 2020 yet? I could go on and on with many others, like the additional 15 Fed Gov Security Agencies responsible for protecting us!

As the late John McCain on the Presidential Committee to Investigate the Challenger Disaster screamed, "I want names, I want names!" I voted for John twice, a true American hero, with great respect for his Wartime service. However, I could not keep from saying to myself, look at a mirror John!

3. Panics: Causes & Effects

"Ready, fire, aim!" Mark Cuban tells the talking heads of FOX News after the POTUS Daily News Conference of 3/20/2020 .

Photo 3.0 Tragic day in NYC World Trade Center Towers 1 & 2 gone in minutes! (NY Times photo)

My first panic occurred in Fall of 1944 when, as a toddler, I experienced our first USA Air Raid Exercise that was held in my hometown in NE PA! All lights needed to be turned off, both inside and outside on the town streets. I could only see the lighted cigarette burning on my Fathers right hand as he puffed away nervously! What was going on I thought? Why was this happening? Was it the Japs? Was it the Germans? How long was this going to happen? Even the radio was silent for the first time at night! This exercise was conducted weekly until each time perhaps hours later the all clear signal was given by a person called the Air Raid Warden.

After the War, I recall buying one of those white Air Raid Warden metal helmets for a buck, it seemed everyone had one!

On a cold February Winter day in 1959, awaiting entry into the US Army as a voluntary draft recruit panic ensued at the local Port Griffith coal mine close to the Susquehanna River flowing North to South through the State of Pennsylvania. Several of my neighbors worked there and the anthracite coal mined was still in high demand for power and heating fuel. Around noontime me and several of my friends, also awaiting service, were alerted to a coal mining accident that just occurred. Word was that the river had entered the mine roof and was flooding the entire coal region.

Hurrying down to see the disaster, we were shocked to see a raging circular flow of water entering a huge hole under the riverbed. 26 miners were still trapped below even though the shaft elevator was still operational. One more time, we witnessed a final effort to go below. Minutes later up it came up with the last of the survivors. My friend's Father, Tommy Burns was among the last ride up. Willy Sinclair, a close neighbor, whose 1950 Black as coal Ford coup that I admired and he kept polished like showroom new, was still AWOL!

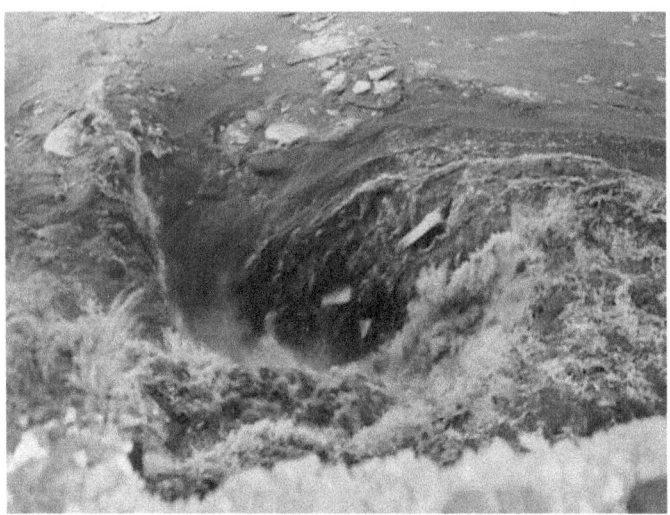

Photo 3.1: Knox Mine Disaster January 22, 1959 (courtesy WNEP.com)

As shown in Photo 3.1 even railroad car after car the Susquehanna River opening devoured them like popcorn at the movie. Railroad ties, like toothpicks made little help when desperate measures of all kinds failed to stop the water from entering the mine!

Into the night, workers and rescue teams were deployed to help with the tragedy.

Photo 3.2. Knox Miners Rescue effort 24 hours later (Citizens Voice Newspaper)

Back to high hill we ran that overlooked the whirlpool-like waterfall, worse there! Attempts to block the flow with train boxcars were of no success. Cautioned by on-site now PA State Troopers to get away from the site and fearing that the hill too would soon be gone we left the scene. Another panic occurred right in my eyesight. By the next day several of the miners escaped finding a local shaft that one climbed out with their bare hands. My recollection was that 12 miners were lost in that disaster.

Our neighbor, Willy was now gone, someone said he was last seen searching for his tool-box before trying to escape! RIP Willy!

In several legal proceedings later, Mine Inspectors were found to be at fault and prosecutions did not replace missing miners, but justice was carried out!

My third panic occurred at 21 years old when as a passenger in a 1955 Chevy upon hitting a telephone pole at 50mph, I hit the windshield (since no safety belts were installed in cars then). Still conscious and bleeding profusely I was taken to the local hospital with no Doctors on duty and was given the last rites of the church.

Fortunately, I recalled a local Doctors name who at 4AM came and saved my life. Yes! I panicked! After serving in the US Army unscratched, I almost bought the farm that night in my hometown.

But who of us WWII born can ever forget that day JFK or RFK was shot...even MLK? Not quite a panic as a great Fall day on September 11, 2001 as I was working at my job at NASA Goddard Space Flight Center, 10 miles from our Nation's Capital, the panic of my lifetime occurred. An attack on America worse than December 7, 1941, Pearl Harbor! 2,977 Americans, mostly civilians, perished in minutes that horrifying day! 6,000 were injured!

On that day 911, 125 were killed just a few miles away at the Pentagon building near the airport in Washington, DC. Most were civilians just doing their jobs! 90 countries lost citizens that fatal day in America. Two massive structures in NYC were gone along with 26 more buildings and their occupants (see Photo 3.0).

Obviously, I survived that panic nearly 20 years ago (although it seems like yesterday) and lived to tell the story and write about it in this new 2020 book and my others too!

Everybody attention!!... We are having an epidemic... perhaps even a pandemic...now everyone panics!

This is what is happening in the timeframe of March 2020 all over the world! People are in a panic state! What to do! What to do! Is on everyone's mind. Our comfort factors are being attacked at a furious rate. Never in modern history have we seen this kind of chaos and right here in the United States of America.

How did it happen: another 911.2, another Pearl Harbor, another crash of 1929.2? Who is responsible? Where was our protection? Where was our systems in place to prevent or mitigate or interdict this kind of chaos?

Living in the most powerful nation on the planet with every possible convenience and every possible protection up to and including our gated communities, somewhere, somehow, out of the blue, an archaic unknown enemy is disturbing our very existence.

I am writing this on March 19, 2020 several days into the abyss. What is happening is beyond our imagination, beyond are in-place controls and systems, both government, military, economic and financial.

How long will it last? Is on everyone's mind. How can it be fixed? Who was responsible? These are questions that go unanswered as of this date. Our leaders every day appear on my high definition 55-inch state-of-the-art 5G television. The expression on their faces does not show confidence. We are not ready for such an unknown attack.

One's mind wonders to similar events that have occurred in our lifetime or in our history books. The plague that occurred worldwide in the year 1918, the attack on Pearl Harbor 1941 and who can forget 911! We will try to answer some of the questions that were just posed. We will delve into the mysteries of epidemics and pandemics of the

20 & 21ˢᵗ Century. Hopefully, what will result are critical lessons learned and systemic fixes to significant gaps in our present government economic and financial systems.

Calendar Day: March 16, 2020,10:30 AM: USA Newspaper Headlines read, **"The day the stock market died!"** Corona virus vs the Planet…Round One!

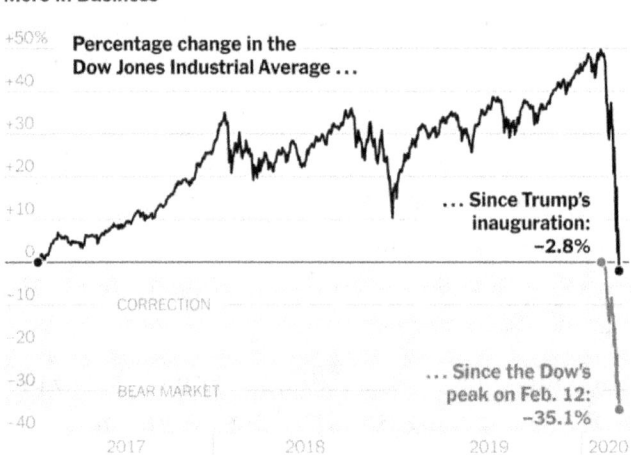

Stock Market's Gain Under Trump Vanishes

Figure 3.3. Trump Wall Street Rally Curve…years of "irrational exuberance"? (NY Times Photo)

As shown in Figure 3.3, called the Trump Wall Street Rally Years, his actions to bring back the old USA to times he grew up in, the last half of the 20th Century. As he says today we are in a *"medical crises not a financial one!"* Regardless of how it is described, however, it is all about money!

Impact: World-wide epidemic 2020: "The sky is falling!" *"We have nothing to fear but fear itself!"* FDR 1933!

And remember Pearl Harbor, December 6, 1941! Other famous quotes made at the time was one made by our then enemy.

"We have unleashed a sleeping tiger by our actions!"
Adm. Yamamoto Japan 1941.

From a purely military viewpoint, surprise is one of our weaknesses since our Country began!

Here we are still resting on our World War II laurels, wondering what is happening almost 70 years after our ongoing historic victories in Europe and Asia. Just over 100 years from the WWI and plague of 1918 when nearly 500,000 in the USA succumbed from that Spanish Flu disease. And 45,000 soldiers overseas. And an estimated 50 million around the world!

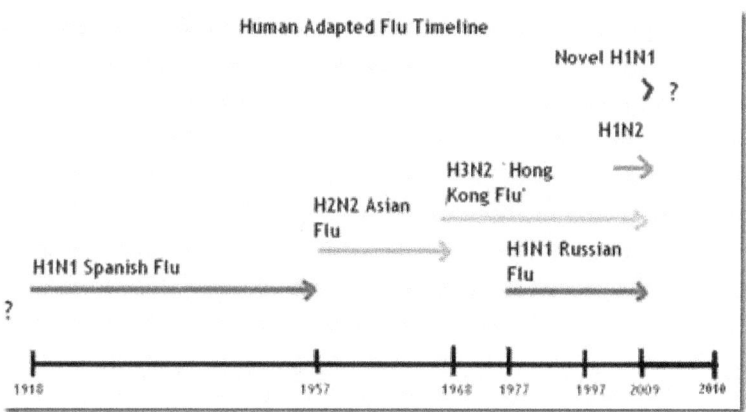

Exhibit 3.4 20th Century Flu timeline.
(afludiary.blogspot.com)

As seen above in Exhibit 3.4, the foreign Flu virus has been around for over 100 years. Perhaps we need to try eliminating origins and focus on developing a generic vaccine that can be adapted to drive to zero infections like we do with "Zero Defects" product defects approach on the frequent annual incidences of occurrence.

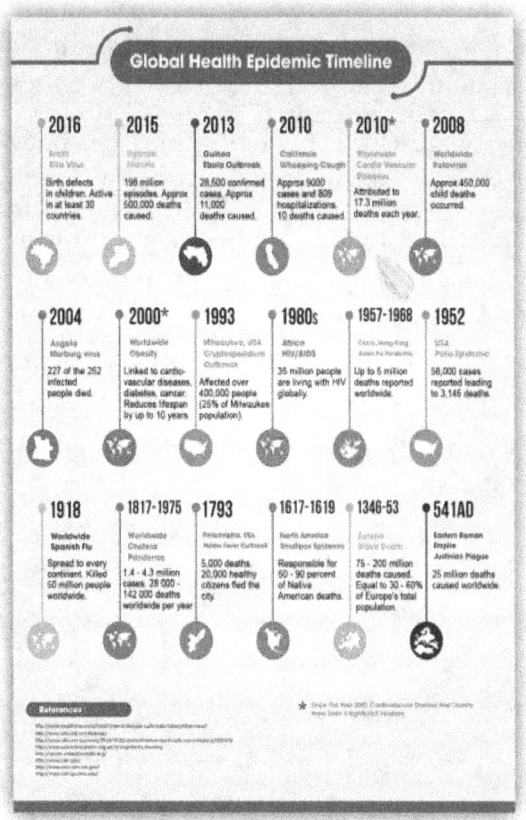

Exhibit 3.5 Global Health Epidemic Timeline Chart (www.fastcoexist.com)

As seen in the above Exhibit 3.5 Globally, 12 Epidemics have occurred since the 1950s:

1. 1952 – Polio: 58,000 cases; 3245 deaths
2. 1967 – Asian, Hong Kong Flu: 5,000,000 deaths
3. 1980s – African HIV/AIDS: 32M died, 35M living!

4. 1983 – Cryptosporidiosis/H20: 400,000 infected in Milwaukee (25% population!)
5. 2000 – World-wide Obesity: 10-year lifetime reduction!
6. 2004 – Angola virus: 227 of 252 people died!
7. 2008 – Rotavirus: 450,000 children died!
8. 2010 – Cardio/Vascular: 17,300,000/Year died!
9. 2013 – CA Whooping Cough: 9.000 cases, 10 deaths, 809 hospitalizations.
10. 2015 – Guinea Ebola: 28,000 cases, 11,000 deaths
11. 2016 – Uganda Malaria: 198M cases, 500,000 dead!
12. 2018 – Brazil Virus: Birth defects, Active in 30 Countries.

As one can see from the above listing, the medical profession is kept terribly busy by around the Planet epidemics. And the frequency of occurrence seems to be climbing exponentially with World-wide jet travel taking one to the other side of the globe overnight!

Note also, that the USA with its many good in-place sanitation, hygiene practices and food distribution networks provides its citizens with a second-to-none nation of healthy and in most cases, wealthy citizens. After travelling to all parts of the World and comparing living conditions, I welcome returning to my safe home called the USA!

The Greatest Generation would rollover in their graves today by observing such 21st-century debacle. Such 20th Century platforms as the quest for socialism and still fighting for civil rights and gender equality. It seems at times that the inmates have taken over our society…the inmates at the insane asylum.

Today's many protestors of oppression take for granted how secure they are in the USA. They, not being satisfied by the amazing results of our capitalist system and seem to be longing for change, at any price, is now being offered. Just, in many cases, to disrupt our way of life. Perhaps it is reflected by today's business books that propose, if it is not broken, break it. Difficult for a kid like me to accept, this new notion, who at my early years was taught to keep things for as long as you can! If I ain't broken, do not fix it!

This rule first was applied to my shoes…resole them over and over, torn jeans….patch them, pencils…sharpen them to the eraser, food left over…tomorrows meal! Plant a Victory Garden if you have some space! Exercise and nutrition at the same time!

I was raised in a "rebel for a cause" era. It was tempered by the military draft and after that, marriage, later and finally just earning a living with several offspring depending on my labors. Not to mention a keep up with the Joneses drive to success. The seeds of unrest are in our DNA! Now, we are being just the new USA visitors, who were replanted and tantalized by New World freedoms. And longing, at times, for returning to our classic European origin countries.

For example, on my last trip to Italy in the center of Florence Square in Italy, I asked myself why I am not living here. This is where my ancestors came, from my native country. What am I doing on the other side of the planet in a place called the USA!

Back to my 2020 reality, a new virus originally named after my favorite pastime drink of the 20th century, Corona! The bubble has burst after 10 years of economic wealth, gone just a few days. Like our computers and high-speed Internet, suddenly dissolved like a puff of smoke and high wind did on March 16, 2020, the second worst day in 124 years, is what the talking heads are saying on TV.

Do not be afraid now, we are going to get somewhat technical to analyze what happened to our defenses in the Panic of 2020. At NASA, I introduced a great tool called Barrier Analysis (Thx. to Dr. Tom Davis MPH) to illustrate system gaps that caused many anomalies and failures. Over the years, using mission after mission Lessons Learned, these gaps were filled by new policies, procedures, training, and even new organizations.

All were specifically designed to deal with new gaps such as those needed by our fixes in place to deal with another Panic 2020!

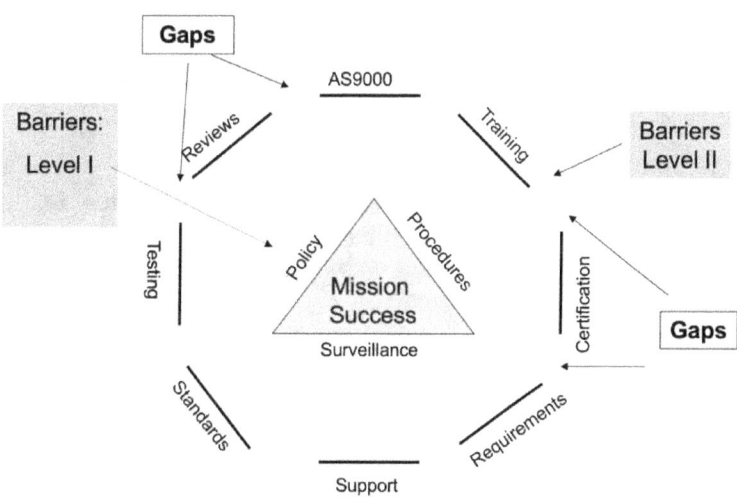

Exhibit A. Bio-threat Agency Prevention, Interdiction, Detection, & Containment

Exhibit A: Barrier Analysis Tool for doing Systems Analysis.

Using a Barrier Analysis analogy and applying it to our Panic 2020 situation many gaps can be found in our present systems. Throughout our vast structure there are many Fed Agencies who can deal with such disasters. FEMA is the first who comes to mind to us all. Specifically, the CDC charter is to cover the bases in dealing with COVID-19 viruses.

Also, Military coverage is out of the DOD, at a large DC operation. On our Agency system side is the Department of Public Health with a Cabinet-based Surgeon General is also involved. Lastly, is the Department of Homeland Security a new one established after 911! And yet, there are still gaps as our Barrier Analysis reveals.

Recently a huge gap was covered in our Space Operations with the launching of the new Space Force! Perhaps such a quasi-military operation is necessary for dealing with these new threats? Perhaps consolidation is necessary, even rightsizing our many Agencies and Operations. As it should be with our 15 Fed Agencies dealing with USA Security.

Even football teams have 11 players and baseball have 9, basketball an amazingly fast paced sport just 5! No one can play or keep score with 15 or more players! The ideal team according to Fayol, a French iconic business-man, the number is 12. And that goes way back thousands of years ago!

Again, it will take a high-level Blue-Ribbon Committee such as the 911 Commission to unravel the Panic of 2020.

Appendix 1, of this book, identifies what is needed to be done and by whom in DC Fed Gov. to fill in the failure gaps!

4. Five W's: Who, When, What, Where, Why & How!

"If you can't learn from history you must repeat it over and over again!" Carlos Santana

Photo 4.1 First ever shutdown of NYC Economy! (NY Times Photo)

Every news reporter learns the 5 W's, a basic requirement in describing any event that may occur and be written as soon as a deadline is noted. The Editor will assure that all W's are answered.

Who: Unknown, invisible killer germ that once acquired results in illness that may be fatal to humans contacting it!

When: Earliest discovery, November 2019 with first victims reported in Wuhan, China!

What: According to CDC.gov, first described as a new corona virus, now identified as COVID-19 that has no known vaccine to prevent infection.

Where: Asian Continent, China city of Wuhan in Hubei Province one of the most popular cities in China!

Why: First indications are animal to human transfer of virus…live "wet" marketplace perhaps a bat source!

How: With today's ability to fly to remote regions of the planet in hours, around the clock, this infection can rapidly be transmitted to every region of human habitation.

As USA newspaper headlines read on April 8, 2020:

The COVID-19 virus may cause 60,415 Americans to lose their lives!

Where do we put our years of "Social Engineering" as a Federal goal driven priority? Those hope and change years now lost in the rear-view mirror. From our drives since our founding for liberty and justice for all starting with the Boston Tea Party. Continuing with our Civil War between the Northern industrial might's against the Southern land and slave holders. On-ward to the race riots and civil rights movement of the 1960s to present LGBTQ Era…but little focus on our ability to preserve the foundations of our republic and democracy was founded, except for the military and industrial complex, so vividly described to us be our great POTUS Eisenhower at the end of his eight year term in 1959!

Let us now look at the life cycle of a pandemic! This was defined by the CDC.

1. Phase 1 – Investigation: Type & Identification?
2. Phase 2 – Recognition: Number of Cases?
3. Phase 2 - Initiation: Confirmation of Cases?
4. Phase 3 – Acceleration: Actions & Closures?

5. Phase 4 - Deceleration: Decreasing number of cases?
6. Phase 5 - Preparation: Monitoring & Risk Assessment

A good analogy was to use the famous economic life-cycle first written by Walt Rostow, OBE, Yale Ph.D., in his five steps to modern world economic growth. From Takeoff to High Mass Consumption!

I too, was shaken by events of the past few weeks. Let us face it, we all were! Admit it! Now like the heavyweight fighter hit by a Rock Marciano hit…you either go down or you do go down for the count. And 1,2,3,4,5,6,7….you stagger up! We Americans staggered up and got our fighting face on. Here is what each sector of our great free prosperous country did!

SAVE YOUR COMPANY is the name of the game for CEOs. The smart ones know that this is a short-term problem. And when things return to an open for business basis, all those workers, who work at home, will be available and will seamlessly return to their workplaces!

Econ 101 educated and trained managers know all about the cost/benefits analysis that will determine the extent of the country shutdown. If misjudged a return, it could drive the country not only into a recession, but more fearfully, a 1929 Depression.

POTUS will not let this happen on his watch. Let us thank Wharton School of Business for providing the ECON 101 training for the POTUS! Therefore, he is forecasting a return to work, at first, perhaps by Easter time. Do the cost/benefit analysis. On one side of the equation you have the shutdown with all cost impacts….add up the numbers worse case wise. Unemployment, lost wages, lost sales, loss taxes, lost investment, bankruptcies…enough yet? Compare this to a return to work side of the coin! Even with the NYC now reaching 6% fatalities at this April 22, 2020 date!

Now, however, we realize the reality of dealing with this deadly COVID-19, when daily 600 to 800 deaths per day die just in NYC, now the USA's Hottest Zone!

Latest Shutdowns now on 4/15/2020 are extended to May 15 by most USA State Governors. Leveling has occurred but at an extremely high level and immunization now appears to be the only long-term solution.

Today, more than ever in my lifetime, I am proud to be an American. Our government finally are returning to their American roots and senses….100%, for many months' adversaries, finally voted for the new $2.2T Recovery Bill !

On March 26, 2020 we saw a third UP day, in a row, of the World Markets! This Stat is a leading economic indicator that for many days is on a positive track. Fed Action, Congressional action, virus news…all cause algorithm trading turns positive.

Dateline: Thursday, March 26, 2020, 11.00AM

Dow - 22,000, up 764

NASDAQ – 7,595, up 213

S&P – 2,564, up 85!

From my March 19, 2020 Diary, **"Stop the bleeding!** I watched for days, when USA Wall Street markets dropped by thousands of points from a high of 30,000 to a present level of 20,000. Over a 10,000-point drop! Ending up at a negative $7 Trillion wealth loss!

Fantasy! No, no…! Reality 2020AD! With little or no government oversight or Wall Street Management intervening. Oh yes, there are so-called market circuit breakers, but never designed for a worldwide pandemic, such an international event so quickly happening.

Sure a few circuit breakers designed for much less serious events occurred at -7%, -12%, and -20%! And as I watched, they were executed over and repeatedly!

You would think that someone, somehow, even the so-called Invisible Hand would have intervened to interdict such irrational behavior! All that was mentioned at the Federal level was "we are going to keep the markets open"! One observer could say "do something even if it's wrong"!

Let us step back however and recall what was done in 1934 because of the Crash of 1929. The big Agency created to deal with Wall Street was the new SEC formed with Boston's Joseph Kennedy at the head. New Rules were imposed on the traders. Margins were adjusted, trading time was shortened. Full disclosure was a requirement.

So, in Wall Street's case what was needed was someone to apply pressure point instant action to save the patient in this case... The United States of America economy from collapse.

Watching Lou Dobbs Fox News on March 16, 2020 again I heard the words "the second worst day in 124 years." Is anyone listening out there? Does anyone know what to do. The patient is in the ER looking for survival! Call for the MDs, call for anyone who knows what to do!

Yesterday was a difficult one for me and my retired friends one of whom lost almost 1 million his 401(k) last week but what about the other 100 million USA members of our 401 community not to mention the 403B folks also.

How difficult is it to lose $100,000 one week? suppose you were 55 save $25,000 per year it would take four years to put that away. And 1 million about 40 years! The 401(k)s started in the 1980s. I started my 1983 and was 40 years ago... A worker's lifetime.

If someone took your 40 years of savings what would you do? Cry? Get drunk? Sue? One cannot recover! Perhaps if you are 21 years of age, you may.

In my case, market losses in the last 2008 crisis took almost 12 years to recover. What will it take to recover from the 2020 tragedy 20? Perhaps 2040 in my 100th year!

As a retired manager, with the Babson MBA (whose college founder saved JFK's father Joe from collapse in the '29 crash) watching the bleeding of our USA economy for the past several days was like seeing a hospital patient in intensive care suffering without treatments and spite of the state-of-the-art facilities available greatest medical professionals at their disposal. And no one acting.

Yes, no one knew how to use a tourniquet or new first-aid or the bodies pressure points! Especially our inept DC politicians were mostly looking for a legal action solution.

Perhaps like the medical profession, it too is entitled, the practice of law or the practice of medicine, all are just practicing!

Stock market circuit breakers of 7%, 12% and 20% would not help stop the bleeding. You would think that someone with common sense would intervene, however, even our US Treasury Secretary had insisted that they keep the market open (for liquidity!) perhaps at any cost, even if there is another 1929 Depression? Don't we expect a better approach to dealing with a runaway stock market sell-off, controlled now by computers…especially for Worldwide Pandemics? US citizens lives are at stake here along with their lifetimes of savings…this is not 1929!

As a college trained professional, I cannot accept this predicament without, somewhat rage…as I am sure you cannot either. Someone, perhaps many in seats of power, must pay dearly for this panic of 2020! Where were the

Titanic lifeboats! While Wall Street was sinking quickly our leaders were re-arranging the deck chairs neatly leading us quickly into the disaster!

And our poor POTUS…so businesslike! A victim of a poor, obsolete governmental system doing the best he could while opposition continuously undermines his every action. And not contributing at all to solving the problem! The DC Beltway big word is referred to as "exacerbation" used when no other sellable solution is available for the confused public and those in charge.

"This too shall pass" is their attitude, as their lifestyles and comfort factors are mildly interrupted. Such is the case in the country whose citizens are told as "the home of the brave and land of the free!"

And on April 15, 2020, only the POTUS and VPOTUS are seen on duty in DC. All the others are still on their Easter vacation!

Ed Note: Today's date 3/20/2020, several US Senators were indicted for selling their stock portfolios just prior to the crash…they sure did not alert me …did they you?

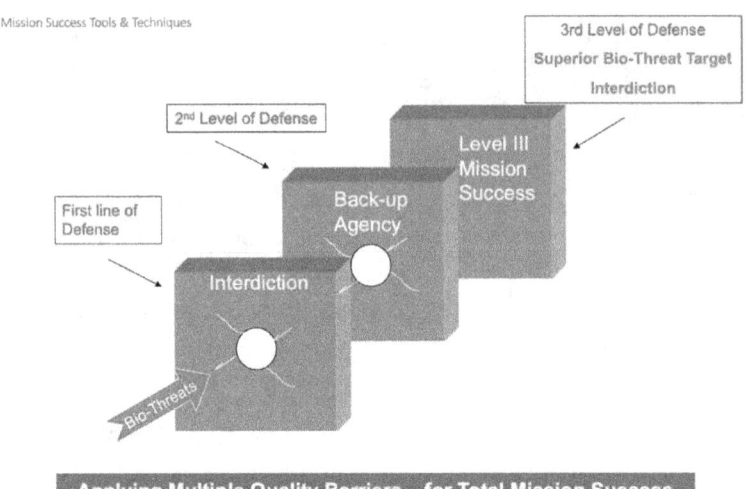

Exhibit 4.0 A systems failure event requires several Barriers to be overcome as the arrow shows. Three Barriers for Bio-threats are illustrated here.

Ed. Note: Imagine the dangers in missing three divided highway Jersey Walls barriers on a now undivided Interstate, as cars fly by at 70 to 80 miles an hour! Thank those Stevens Institute folks for that life-saving invention!

In analyzing the Panic of 2020, several missing USA Defensive Barriers were needed to be overcome the threats as Exhibit 4.0 so vividly displays. First, the element of surprise was needed, that occurred. Initial news reports were that the virus was not contagious, we fell for that.

Our many Security Agencies (13 by my last count, not counting the four military) again, same as 2001 did not connect the dots. Perhaps they were focused on the Middle East, or like we were in 911, still fighting the Cold War with the Russians! Or doing more impeachment searches as was going on at this critical time in the USA!

The Second Barrier to be overcome was <u>time</u>. This too was not handled well to say the least. Once cross contamination and the contagion was discovered the USA should have been in lockdown with all international travelers. No Plans were initiated…because there was no plan! According to POTUS, he needed to make that decision based on his own "gut feel"!

POTUS Trump over and over admits what we had in place, were systems designed to address small threats. No Pandemic warfare games, or Pandemic models were developed in our many Agencies that may have been once played, yielded a step by step nationwide defense plan. However, we made one along the way and it still under development as a Works-in-Progress, as they say, inside the DC Beltway.

The third barrier can be answered by one question? Where is the <u>accountability</u>? Again like 911, this is difficult to answer. The novice might blame the Chinese, the Drug cartels, the Democrats? Fox TV Star Ms. Trish Reagan apparently paid dearly for that one, got fired, and we all miss her!

Let us look inside, who, what agencies or agencies are chartered to protect us from a Pandemic…you got it, no Agency has primary charter to defend and protect us from this invisible force. Now some say, wait a minute, what about the CDC, **WHO, UN**, FEMA, US Public Health Service?

Just WHO is WHO? Well, they are part of the UN, based in Geneva, Switzerland. The folks who raised hell over the China travel ban when it was initiated by our POTUS. And secondly, told us initially there was no human contagion! And, later changing their mind on both subjects. Need I go further? Look them up at Google!

As time goes on now, into the Month of April, April 8, 2020 to be exact, the dots are beginning to show. Cause and effect relationships are being finally questioned.

I high-lighted two acronyms in my first list of usual suspects…UN & the WHO!

Thousands of victims could have been saved if accurate reporting of the seriousness of the virus was quickly communicated. It appears that initial transmissions occurred in Wuhan, China mid-December 2019. And remember the 14-day window of incubation. Perhaps a start date could have been occurring in November 2019.

Wikipedia web-site correlates with my origin and timeframe estimation. See:

(https://en.wikipedia.org/wiki/Timeline_of_the_2019%E2%80%9320_coronavirus_pandemic_from_November_2019_to_January_2020).

At that time, the month of November 2019 in Wuhan, China, capital of Hubei Province, many important worldly meetings were held there. The City has a population of over 11 million, somewhat equal with the USA Boston/Washington (BoWash) corridor!

International Conferences held in China goes back for years…even the Fortune 500 annual meeting was held years ago in Chengdu, China a city of 15,000,000 located in the southern, middle part of the country, in Sichuan Province.

Direct flights were flown from Washington DC non-stop to this location about 8,000 miles from our capital of DC!

Did you know that China now surpasses the USA in the Fortune's Global 500? Yes, the USA American Companies total 121, China 129 (including 10 Taiwanese companies)!

I recall on my first trip to Hong Kong and visiting the industrial district of Shenzhen, just a short train trip away. Upon entering the city, and staying at the luxurious Shangri La Hotel, it was far superior in style, comfort, and amenities to any recent NYC one.

Upon entering, I was surprised to see Western businessmen enjoying their Happy Hour drinks while watching and listening to American Jazz tunes sung live by a beautiful girl dressed in a sequenced, glittering long, formal gown like she was celebrating New Year's Eve in NYC. To me, it was like a scene out of a Bogart movie of the 1940s. China had finally arrived at the 20th, perhaps 21st Century.

Two important events happened in Wuhan during this October/November timeframe. The first in October, a 2019 International Conference on Human Health and Medical Engineering (HHME2019), Wuhan, China, 27–28 October 2019.

Secondly, another one, Quark Matter 2019 - the XXVIIIth International Conference on Ultra-relativistic Nucleus-Nucleus Collisions - 3-9 November 2019 Wanda Reign Wuhan Hotel.

Perhaps these were attended by Western World attendees and could have become carriers going back to their native lands, again, just perhaps?

5. Business, Industry & Government Impact

"The American Republic will endure until the day Congress discovers that it can bribe the public with the public's money!" Alexis de Tocqueville (1805-1859)

Photo 5.0 Rare sight of empty NYC in Panic 2020! (NY Times Photo)

The big picture of our capitalist system is made up by three major sectors: Business (Fortune 500), Industry (Manufacturing, Services) and finally our Governments (Federal, State, County, and local Municipalities). Together they make up the engines, driving forces that provides for our safety, security and protection from chaos that was part of our long ago, Wild West Era.

What occurs when our stability is disturbed as in national disasters happens? What results can be a short or long-term duration. Short-term is less than one-year timeframe. Long term is greater than one-year timeframe.

OK now! Let us start using our heads…instead of losing it! Put on your USA hat! Trust the leader who keeps his head when all others are losing theirs! Will, imagination, reason and finally judgement need to all be used to work out any problem or situation or panic!

Use your street smarts, training, education, experience that is in your mind's toolbox! What applies here? Hint: USA economy/financial markets….oh yes! Economics! Let us look deeper in the toolbox….here it is a great tool…Cost-Benefit Analysis! Yes, this will help put some light on the subject!

After a Google search to refresh my thoughts as to creating a model, I discovered a great article that hit the nail on its head. National Review 3/23/2020 article "A COVID Cost Benefit Analysis" by Robert Verbruggen. Let us look at this in further detail and see what is revealed…so clearly! Thanks Robert!

First, to do a Cost Benefit Analysis (CBA) one needs many inputs that are called variables. And a formula to determine the solution. Cost/Benefits! Here are just a few needed variables described in the NR article:

   a. *number of casualties*
   b. *number of asymptomatic*
   c. *doing absolutely nothing*

  d. *taking some minimal steps*
  e. *gross national product or GNP*
  f. *number of lives saved*
  g. *healthcare costs*
  h. *damage to economy people hospitalized*
  i. *misery of being intubated*
  j. *patients not being intubated (ventilators not available)*
  k. *short-term hit on the GNP, huge new government spending*
  l. *Cost of preserving the benefits*
  m. *frustration and mental health problems (being unemployed/cabin fever)*
  n. *future economic damage*
  o. *human capital/student/worker atrophy*
  p. *counterfactual*
  q. *social distancing costs*
  r. *value of statistical life – $9,000,000*
  s. *quality adjusted life years - $125,000*

….Need a computer now… you betcha! Where are you Boston Colleges Computer Consortium? Harvard, MIT, BC, UMass, Northeastern, Babson, etc, etc.

Reality check now...obviously, not all variables are available to complete our model or will they ever be! So, as Robert, the fine gentleman author says: "let's try it anyway with what we can estimate!" Here goes…

Casualties – Imperial College Model – USA 2,000,000 (if we do nothing). If we do some mitigation – 1,000,000!
USA GDP – Goldman Sacks est. $4T/QTR; drop 24%/QTR; $21T/YR.; $5T/QTR. Article used $1.5T!
USA FED Relief - $6T Phase one! $2T +$4T!
Lives Saved – Yield decade of life at 78! 1,000,000

Cost for Preserving - $1.25T
Formula & Results:
    Option A: Cost/Benefit = $1.25T/1,000,000 lives saved.
    Answer is, Option B: Cost/Benefit = $5T/QTR/329,000,000 American survivors!

And now let us look at more statistics. After plugging in the raw data into our magic machines, we can look at some information results and prognostications by our high technology computer models.

Besides the London Imperial College Model that we cited earlier there are many more at play looking at best case and worse case scenarios.

The computer model used by the POTUS Committee is from the Institute for Health Metrics & Evaluation (IHME). Their web site is www.healthdata.org! Latest information declares 12 day until COVID-19 peaks, April 15, 2020 (original Tax Day USA…temporarily moved until July 15, 2020!). Until then, social distancing will remain in effect beyond for 15 more days.

Draconian measures are taking place all over the USA. Masks once mentioned as useless are now the rage. But few can be bought by the uninformed and confused public. Amazon ran out days ago! As well as Home Depot and Lowes! PPE is now the new acronym mantra…personal protection equipment!

Let us look more at the IHME Computer model statistical graphs, tables, and amazing charts. Here we go readers…..and remember these are interactive and updated daily…what is displayed is web-site results dated 4/4/2020.

COVID-19 Projections

GHDXVIZ HUB

COVID-19 projections assuming full social distancing through May 2020

**As the pandemic progresses, we are working to incorporate new data about the virus in the US.
Please check back on Saturday, April 4 for our next update.**

Last daily update on April 1, 2020.

FAQ | Update Notes | Article

Hospital resource use

11days

until peak resource use on

April 15, 2020

Resources needed for COVID-19 patients on peak date

All beds needed

262,092beds

Bed shortage

87,674beds

ICU beds needed

39,727beds

ICU bed shortage

19,863beds

Invasive ventilators needed

31,782 ventilators

○ All resources　○ All beds　⊙ ICU beds　○ Invasive ventilators

0 50k 100k 150k 200k 250k 300k 350k 400k 450k Resource count Mar 01 Apr 01 May 01 Jun 01 Jul 01 Aug 01 Date

All beds needed (projected)
ICU beds needed (projected)
Invasive ventilators needed (projected)
Shaded areas indicate uncertainty

Deaths per day

12 days

until projected peak in daily deaths

2,644 COVID-19 deaths

projected on April 16, 2020

0 500 1k 1.5k 2k 2.5k 3k 3.5k 4k 4.5k Deaths per day Mar 01 Apr 01 May 01 Jun 01 Jul 01 Aug 01 Date

Deaths per day
Deaths per day (projected)

Total Deaths

93,531 COVID-19 deaths

projected by August 4, 2020

0 20k 40k 60k 80k 100k 120k 140k 160k 180k Total deaths Mar 01 Apr 01 May 01 Jun 01 Jul 01 Aug 01 Date

Total deaths
Total deaths (projected)
Shaded area indicates uncertainty

Institute for Health Metrics and Evaluation

Wow! Thanks so much, University of Washington and IHME! So many stats for all the USA public to digest. Great Job Folks!

Think about what is going on and it seems on and on, no one goes out and we all hunker down, talk to no one live, meet no one new, soon it will flatten the curve. The medical community on TV says it will. But only time will tell! Ok, but, for how long?

Day 17 of the stay at home Fed Gov order. All states now on board with the DC attempt to level out the curve as they say. In my native State of PA cities are now asking for National Guard help in keeping the peace. Curfews are imposed keep people off the streets at night!

Latest national news on 4/4/2020 this PM announces re-opening Cheyenne Mountain Military Complex home of NORAD and USNORTHCOM Headquarters are located. The charter of this Complex is to provide aerospace warning and air sovereignty and protection of the Northern USA.

And recall the Naval Armata sent last week by the POTUS to South American territories! Perhaps there is more to this Panic of 2020 that yet is to be revealed! Later we will cover this in much more detail!

6. Global: Social/Economic/Political & Legal Shock

"We shall fight them on the beaches, on the shores, in the air, on the land, on the water....and we will never, never give up our lands, possessions or natural God given rights!" Paraphrasing Sir Winston Churchill (1874-1965) famous speech of WWII!

Photo 6.0 NYC Subway on rare occasion, empty of souls. (NY Times Photo)

In the US, the second greatest generation is now retiring or retired. Our can-do culture was handed off the ball from the World War II, Korea and now Vietnam Patriots, who swore an oath of allegiance to protect the United States of America, a key cultural human resource is now also gone!

This leaves us with their offspring Generation X, Y, and the new generation… Z. There lies a big gap in difference in cultures.. These are the new Americans, all seeking to reach the highest levels of self-actualization!

As a World War II born American. I was exposed to a quite different way of life. As kids, we practiced war games since all our fathers were overseas. We carried on the struggle to achieve the American dream, in turn, it was our job to own a home, raise a family, enter the workforce. Now gone from our presence, but not from our minds, were our veteran Dads. Onward to the high technology challenges of tomorrow. I started working computers in the early 1970s.

Microsoft was formed in Boston in that era with Bill Gates and software experts from Honeywell. Steve Jobs and found work for a summer at HP. And after was told to come back after he gets his BSEE at Stanford. Little did they know at the time, that one day, Apple would be a bigger company formed without his Stanford degree! The same story, without degrees, are entrepreneurs, Bill Gates and Larry Ellis, CEO of Oracle. I could go on and on how without a college degree, they all made it big!

Our World War II baby offspring's generation went to educational institutions that were at the time, number one in the world! We watched as our USA education ranking went downward from 9 to 15 to 20 and now 27! Our ally, South Korea has been number one in mathematics for the past 10 years. I was shocked to see how much decline in education occurred while, at the same time, we were number one in funding education.

What does this mean? Are we going to be numbered 30 or number 40 soon? Compare my culture with the culture of today. Each day upon arriving at grade school, we were first exposed to reading the Bible. Next, we made a Pledge of Allegiance to the flag! Oftentimes, we followed by singing the Star-Spangled Banner or America the Beautiful! This was done daily, not just at athletic sports and special occasions! Few today even know the words to any of these patriotic tunes!

Remember we were the winners both the European and Asian campaigns. Our fathers came home to large celebrations decorated with many of their honors of battles won! Yes, we were the enlightened winners in all our endeavors from sports to work and even play! And honors were given to our American heroes throughout our society.

Today radical change has taken place in our culture and society from pre-school to kindergarten, grade school to colleges our entire USA educational systems. Even in sports, just participating in the endeavor can yield you an award or trophy. Everybody wins and everybody passes! Perhaps, many of the reasons for our country being number 27 in education instead of number one!

Day 20 of the Panic of 2020, Friday, March 20. From my diary, medical workers today are screaming, "the sky is falling"! Physical distancing is now the name of the game! And remember years ago, when gas was below two-dollars a gallon, today again it is less in 19 states! Stock market futures, however, are up today! And the Bank of America says they are going to defer mortgage payments!

All retail sales are noticeably quiet; however, Amazon still is the choice for on-line purchases. That is helping the economic situation, especially for small businesses connected to the world-wide web!

Be careful TV and internet ads say, fake corona tests are now offered even through robocalling, to take your money. Fake websites selling supplies, fake tests, even emails are becoming filled with trash ads.

Several US senators are today indicted for selling stock before the current crash! The usual excuses are given, of no knowledge of them knowing, it was their fiduciary to blame! However, we all wish we had those large broker accounts with safety margin computer-driven sell orders and the same inside connections! But our 401K accounts do not provide that option! They never did by design!

The state of Kentucky declared martial law starting today. However, the liquor stores remain open the result of powerful liquor lobby in the state! They will even deliver cases of beer to your home. Hea, PA Governor why close all those State-run Liquor Stores. Oh yes, more Federal funds can be given, if they are closed…did not think of that scheme!

A new word is being circulated as levels "devolve" to a lower level form. A new, centralized government is then created to preserve continuity of government. This is built into Fed Disaster Plans should it be necessary to close DC!

Perhaps DC is to pick surviving US based companies since one estimates a 30% employment rate. Perhaps 80% of New York enterprises will get the record unemployment that could exceed 30%!

As of today, 4/17/2020, 22,000,000 are claiming for unemployment assistance! How long can funds last is being questioned and what about the retired folks how long can SS last? Estimates say that for every month like this, two year of SS are lost. Now estimated to be in 2033 instead of 2035! DC is sending out feelers about cutting by 25% todays SS just to save the Fund! WE are being described as non-producers as they use our funds to cope with the panic like LBJ first did to pay for the Viet Nam War!

The Federal Government is deadlocked on a bill to fix the economy! The invincible enemy is arriving nationwide, and people has been stopped gathering, to flatten the curve decline and incantation. The USA is disappearing right before eyes. Even the word depression is heard. More Draconian levels are being spoke about this week.

How long does the POTUS have? And the other 534 Federal Government Representatives? Again, how long did he have? For you intelligent readers, perhaps we can do 30 days or maybe 45 days certainly not 90!

Why you say?

"Put yourself into the shoes of a Russian peasant in the 1890s!" As said by Dr. Cristy, Prof. NYU, who was lecturing to us in my first Contemporary Society 101 course at Fairleigh Dickinson University in Teaneck, N J in 1967.

There we were most of us Military Veterans attending our first college classes under the new G.I. Bill signed by POTUS LBJ.

Just before we started losing over 58,000 GIs under his watch in the War of Viet Nam (November 1, 1955 – April 30, 1975)!

Nine-millions of us served on active duty, 2,709,918 served in VN, 543,482 served at the peak, 58,202 KIA and 303,704 wounded. MIA 2338!

So, I ask you once again to put yourself into the shoes of a USA blue-collar pickup truck owner with a shotgun on the rear window. Or veteran of our latest no-win Wars? How long do they have? For that matter how long do we all have? I and my WWII peers are in our last quarter of our lifecycle!

Back to our question? How long do the 535 US Government officials have before chaos ensues in reaching a point of no return in the minds of most Americans?

As our model shows and a cost-benefit analysis so certainly occurs before the end of 2020. So, let us go back. Start with September 2020, one according to some model's shutdown chaos will be rampant! Martial law will then be in effect. Foods shortages will appear. Bottle water perhaps may no longer exist. Gas stations are closed and like World War II rationing stamps are required just to get a gallon of gas.

Unacceptable you say, yes unacceptable! Next, let us visit ahead, August 2020. Big populations are beginning to lose control, escaping to other places on earth is no longer an option!

But our offspring the generation XYZ want to live for a long time!

Back to my generation who, up this date March 30, 2020, have spent weeks under quarantine! And the 330 million of us in 50 states who have been hunkered down too! For starting weeks ago, my wife and I prepared for at least a 2 to 4-week shutdown. After that? Who knows, no more water? No more Bread? Shortages are sure to occur!

Gas is already down to $1.50 a gallon, here in the Sunshine state. In Tennessee, where my son lives, it is down to $.99 a gallon, a 1970 level just after the OPEC oil embargo. It was just 0.33 cents per gallon on one day, 1.00 the next, in 1973! Nixon wanted to send in the US Marines to take the oil-fields but had his hands full dealing with the Watergate Scandal! Today, oil at $20 a barrel, down from 60, as the entire industry is glutted with supply! Oil nations are turning off the spigot as fast as possible.

You saw the pictures of many places in the USA, we never had an international shutdown.

As a young man first entering the work world, in the military, my eye was on by those high-level persons. At the time, US Army's officers such as: Majors and Colonels, were some of these first earning my respect. Even Green Beret Airborne Ranger Officers were to be looked up to and respected. Not to mention those West Point cadets attending the same electronic schools and running in formation all over the base.

As I entered the private sector, I was exposed to many high-level executives even the great ones, like Bill Hewlett and David Packard, ICONIC Founders of HP and my first technical job. And an NH, High-Tech ICON Royden Sanders, CEO who brought 10,000 of us to his Granite State of NH in the 1960s!

Today even after POTUS Trump, it takes a lot for me to have that same feeling. No longer do I naïvely accept those from the Ivy League schools with such admiration. I fear for America, for our survivors, for our future.

After reading Lee Iacocca's book ***"Where Have All the Leaders Gone?"*** in the Election Year of 2016, and applying his criteria, I had some difficulty listing anyone of our many candidates as acceptable? Look at the trade-offs, we have made in accepting mediocrity! Can you name some true American leaders out of the significant 535 in DC? Yes, you can, but with many tradeoffs! So, what has changed? Our values, our tastes, our upbringing, our situations, our culture? Yes, I say all the above!

Even the best-case models predict near 100,000 Americans will perish from COVID-19? Was there a COVID-18, I ask? 17,16, 15….? Dr. Anthony Fauci admits based on his guestimate over 100,000 will perish! His colleague, Dr. Deborah Birx, (Rtd. US Army Colonel) Penn Stater, of National Institute of Health (NIH) are the decision-makers in these making these predictions and conclusions.

The "Planning Model" from the Health Institute for Metrics and Evaluation (IHME) shows that 84,000 will perish through August 2020 with a peak occurring the third day after Easter (April 15, 2020)! For my native state of PA, 3,000 deaths and a $540 Billion dollar hit on the economy.

In 2007, a book entitled "***Black Swan***" was written by author Nassin Taleb, NYU Professor of Risk Management. On 3/30/2020, he was being interviewed on Bloomberg TV. I watched with interest as he indicated that today's panic was not a Black Swan situation but a White Swan Event.

According to Google, a Black Swan event, is a metaphor event that comes as a surprise, has a major effect then is "inappropriately" rationalized after the fact, with the benefit of hindsight.

In ancient times, thinking, at the time, was that black swans did not exist, however. this was discounted after black swans were discovered. Let us review the impact on the global economy such as the 2020 pandemic. Black swans are extremely rare, they cannot be predicted, and they cause much damage to the economy.

After a 50-year career working with the best knowledge workers on the planet I have raised the bar for our so-called leaders higher and higher. I cannot on one-hand put the number of superstars, perhaps on the second hand "several others who were "runner ups! In my hands-on professorial duties interfaced with hundreds of graduate-level students taking my courses. Is it me or is it my generation? I asked several of them and they are in complete agreement. It is my generation of now Senior citizens.

We expect excellence in business, government, society and even religion! Remember, we are all from the hard-working post-World War II generation school before grade-flation. And awards were for the exceptional, rather than just participation! No Dr. Timothy Learys in my growing up years.

Do work and you got paid whether it be washing cars as a teenager or helping my father do electrical work since I could almost walk.

I recall even as a teenager watching Bishop Fulton Sheen on TV, now there was a leader. His business was the saving of souls! Certainly, USA leaders were my father's generation like JFK even Richard Nixon comes to mind along with Eisenhower, Reagan, and Truman.

They all took us through those trying times years that occurred during their tenure in the Presidency of the United States! Where are all these leaders when we need them? What happened? Did we stop making them? The Lee Iacocca's, the Billy Graham's, the George S Patton's of the Greatest Generation?

Ok, I got it! After taking my daily bike ride in the somewhat reduced Florida like summer heat, and thanks to my oblique thinking technique taught to me by my Creative Decision-Making Course (CDM), I found the answer to our Leadership quest. Thanks, Northeastern University/Babson College for your training. The answer is **"The Law of Diminishing Returns!"**

Perhaps this is only my perception and my generation! For when you have seen the best in sports for example, the Mantles, DiMaggio, Berra's, Fords, Ruth's, Robinson's, Aarons, Williams….we use them as our standard for comparison …and yes, they become our new high bars or rungs on the ladder of life!

Our off-springs, not seeing and knowing these heroes of the past and their impact on their chosen careers, one cannot appreciate their value in one's judgement.

So, today, we must look for substitutes and make comparisons and yield to new results! For the past is the past! And the present is the present! And the future is the future!

> ***Ed Note:*** I did think of one example where this Law may not apply. With Diamonds! And I did conduct an experiment. For example, years ago, on one trip to The International Mall in Orlando, FL, with my close and recently divorced too friend and pal Frank, we met a beautiful salesgirl who was just engaged.
>
> Wow! We said, "what a beautiful ring?" How many Karats? One, two? She replied, only one. And Frank replied, what if one of us was to offer you two or even three? She waited, thought, with what looked like using all her might, and replied, YES! I would take it!

So sometimes, in human endeavors, more is more…never forget that! I put that true story in just to amuse you reader, no offence intended!

Calendar Day Monday, March 30, 2020! Today, the Federal Government took its first step to remedy the pain of the panic of 2020. A $2.2 trillion dollar (that is 12 zeros!) Rescue Package for the US economy! Not a Financial stimulus, but a Medical one according to our POTUS.

So, what did the House of Representatives folks inside the Beltway, the 435 give their 100 Senate colleagues to work on…? Nothing to fix the problem! No analysis was conducted or done to prevent another panic! No action like there was at done at the turn of the century to prevent more foreigners from bringing to the USA new diseases. Our ancestors came into the USA through rigid medical screening at Ellis Island. Many were sent back as a result.

Perhaps we need to have the same action done today! Just a thought!

Oh yes, US SOS made sure of adding $25 million to the COVID-19 Bill for coping with the virus, almost a $5,000 a month raise for the 435 members, just before leaving DC and flying on her USA Air Force 3, for her well-deserved, Easter vacation!

SS folks like me, got no raise on our future SS checks, perhaps not even a COLA built into the formula! Kind of gives me that "deplorable" feeling, doesn't it you?

Yes zero, all corrective action is again the same old same old fixes… throw dollars at the problem and hope it will go away.

Using partisan platform solutions some of which are favorite things like the arts, I too love PBS! Kennedy Center $35 million (and upon receipt laying all employees off) and local colleges, and other platform priorities such as eliminating voter identification mail in voter measures, etc.. Senior citizens got zero! Yes! They got zero! And they did not call it financial aid just medical funding.

What should we expect? Trained lawyers use new laws as their fixes such are modern-day remedies and new regulations and more documentation, always a good backup and Plan B for DC!

No money to fix the root cause of the problem in this latest invisible enemy. See the following web-site on the $2.2 trillion bill +$4T for the Federal Reserve.
  https://home.treasury.gov/policy-issues/cares

In 2015, five years ago, we had a golden opportunity to prevent today's COVID-19 Pandemic. This was not a 911 situation, as that was surprise attack! At that time, the Gates Foundation spent over $100,000,000 fighting this dreaded disease. Bill Gates himself warned us on video, on the WWW and in books. His March CNN Special revealed all he did to prevent 2020 panic from happening. I watched it in dis-belief!

My question today is why did not we do something at that time to come up with an immunization? Remember POTUS Trump was not elected until November 2016 and was told his biggest threat was Korea!

Where were the thousands in DC Agencies responsible for this situation? Why did it not get fixed with the $100 Million? Look what the opportunity cost, cost us and the USA trillions of dollars and no solution yet!

And another reported in April revelation on COVID-19 is that the good old USA even funded the Wuhan Chinese Laboratory $3.7 million for bat virus research? Most will say never, I know this….never… same as heard in 911 when it was reported that we funded 911 by giving Osama Bin Laden almost $300M in US aid!

Doing a Root Cause Analysis, a common tool used in conducting engineering investigation into failures is exceedingly difficult to determine in any accident situation, let alone with the first modern era pandemic! At NASA we did quite a few from Apollo to Challenger to Columbia disasters. Amazing write-ups are available on-line at: nasa.gov!

7. TRUMP's Wall Street Rally 2016 – 2020

"We are going to Make America Great Again"!
POTUS Trump USA 2016 Campaign theme.

Wilkes-Barre, PA, the Summer of 2016, Election Year, when a packed-house Ice Hockey Arena filled with overflow crowds, broke records for any event. Not even Elvis, in his prime, in 1957, could have gathered such a welcoming audience. Even after filling up the place, many folks, perhaps thousands, lined up outside just to say they were there. No political candidate except for in local cities, who welcomed JFK in 1960, when his convertible car was almost destroyed by the screaming crowds.

Trump's visit illustrated that the USA was hungry for new leadership that reflected their new desires.

For this area, it was Jobs, Money, Safety & Social Security/Medicare/Medicaid and return to an earlier period when pride in a winning America was riding high. Hope and change just did not seem to be the answer in NEPA! DC, all talk, no action words resonated with this mostly blue-collar community crowds.

My attendance was at the insistence of my patriotic wife, Julie, who just earned her USA citizenship after months of preparation and filling out forms, taking tests and high costs of completing the process! USA Citizenship is not free or cheap as we soon found out! Trips to Philadelphia and early morning appointments, tolls, parking fees (25% tax), hotel fees, meals, all need payment before even testing begins. Our costs were in the thousands of USA $$.

We taxpayers (only 50% of us pay Federal taxes) have lost millions of USA $$ revenue by allowing millions of illegals avoiding paying for this process. According to latest statistics we have 12 million of illegals in the home of the free and brave. Do the math!

Todays Fed Gov expert's unemployment future estimates range from 20 to 30%! Recall that the Crash of 1929 our rate was about 20%...hard to imagine 30%! Depression era photos of long breadlines and a cashless population in rags, for clothes…no ATMs then! Right out of the movie entitled "The Grapes of Wrath"!

Photo 7.0 Trump Rally in the Arena, Wilkes-Barre, PA 2016

As you can see by our photo my wife Julie and I arrived early to obtain a good seat for viewing the special event. I have been many rock concerts in my life….the Stones…several times and yes….Tina Turner perhaps 4 or 5, I cannot recall them all. But that was World Class Rock stars!

Sitting before us were many of what appeared to me as Grand Parents…over 50 in age certainly! All with grey hair or was it blue? I asked them who are you folks, they replied we are "Democrats for Trump"!

The results later showed that they were telling the truth! For the Don, as we older people called him, won the Democrat state of PA by their votes….28,000 of them, beating Hillary in her Father's home state. She won Scranton by 2,000 votes, but lost Wilkes-Barre by over 20,000! And lost the great keystone state of Pennsylvania, USA!

Photo 7.1 Trump supporter and my cheerleader at Rally 2016

Afterward, Trump came back several times to the great state of PA again to packed houses with overflow crowds. It was like seeing a free Las Vegas show….unheard of in a national election…even Eisenhower, JFK, Reagan campaigns…a new movement in the USA.

The mantras were the same, now memorized by the crowds like a Rolling Stones concert singing "you can't always get what you want!"

Build that Wall! Lock her up! Drain that Swamp! Closing remarks then chant "We will make America Great Again" We will make America rich again, we will make America Safe again! And in later rallies, we will "Keep America Great Again!

What I saw was like no other political movement ever in the USA. What a night! I have been to many concerts before and paid heavy fees to attend. But this was free…like a Las Vegas show right here in River City. And this continued here several times during that campaign. And, later, the unbelievable results in key Electoral College states again and again right up to midnight of the Election eve in November 2016. Down by some polls by 30% or more, the Heartland of America gave the Presidency to Donald J. Trump!

Being a snowbird, since retiring years ago, we watched the Election results in the early morning hours of November 6, 2016. Florida looked like it was going for the wife of our former POTUS Clinton. She captured her party's nomination after gathering what was called Super Delegates…enough to give her a wire to wire win for her Party.

At the time she polled as the winner in poll after poll across the USA. She won the popular vote at almost 68 million votes over her opponents 64 million votes. But since we are a Republic, smaller states had somewhat more power than larger ones as far as the voter was concerned. About 3:30AM with much TV talking heads, coughing, and choking, the results were in…Florida, with the panhandle vote tilted the win for Trump! North Carolina, South Carolina Democrat strongholds went for Trump. Michigan, Ohio, Minnesota also went Trump! Finally, Wilkes-Barre, PA totals came in almost 28,000 Democrats for Trump….now the declared winner of the Election of 2016! Trump lost Scranton by just 2,000 votes, a since FDR and JFK Democrat strong hold.

What was it that almost 63 million voters who voted for Trump in the heartland of America knew? That the 68 million of the coastal states from all New England to Jersey, NY, MD on the east coast to California's 20 million on the west coast did not know?

Here are my two cents on that subject. I loved Palo Alto, California, later called Silicon Valley, when I lived there in the middle 1960s. And HP was the best hi-tech place on the planet to be employed. The people were the best I ever met also. No backstabbers there like NY/NJ! Everyone I interfaced was treated with respect. One's origin, background and territory did not matter. Even I as a PA coal-cracker native was welcomed to the Golden State!

One of my best technical skill teachers was a native Mexican born gentleman, now US Citizen, who had much better skills and knowledge than I or any of my classmates processed and demonstrated! For some products, only he could overhaul the difficult to produce HP instruments!

No need for affirmative action there, for HP was made up of just hard-working intelligent Americans from every race and culture. It was a delight to learn my chosen trade there. And my electronics trade theory was taught, practiced and even theoretical complex formulas were explained and shown on every blackboard I recall seeing there.

In the Machine Shop at HP on Page Mill Road, hung the sign that read **"Goldwater in '64, Bread and Water '65. No water '66…Bury Goldwater!"**

Independent to say the least, like the Sooners too, intelligent, before the drug culture took over, sober, friendly, and again, hard-working…just a few traits folks there displayed.

People seeking high levels of self-actualization, rather than for just food, clothing and shelter and were more than satisfied in their lifestyles. That was the Golden State in the early stages of development. Ronald Reagan was a result of that era. Once elected Governor of State in financial distress, he asked the States' best businesspeople to go to Sacramento, the Capital, and brainstorm how to get and keep the State out of financial disaster. After 10 days of them working, he implemented all their over 300 recommendations immediately!

That was California in the Governor Reagan years. A visit today to his Semi Valley Library is one to behold. One wonders how they ever got his Boeing 707 up that high hill to his Presidential Library there. American ingenuity at its best!

Table 7.2 Trump Rally Statistics: Wikipedia, Est.

Number of Rallies	Total Attendees	Primary Attendees	General Attendees
Total: 323	1,440,000	790,000	650,000
Primary 186			
General 137			

Note: My conservative estimate is over 3,000,000 based on 10,000/rally!

For your reading pleasure, I looked up the results of the Trump Rally attendance before and after the Primary and General Campaigns In the one we attended, held over 10,000 with thousands more outside.

And remember 63,000,000 Americans voted for Trump, 66,000,000 voted for his opponent. However, Electoral College was 304 to 227. 30 USA States went for Trump, 20 for his opponent! Thanks SIRI!

8. USA "Make America Rich Again" Dream?

"We are going to Make America Rich Again!"
POTUS Trump's USA Campaign speech mantra.

Figure 8.0 Trump Rally (yes, that is him and my favorite star) in the Arena at Wilkes-Barre, PA in 2016…look at that crowd…nearly all Democrats, now Trumpocrats!!

Yes, we were resonating with the new candidates' words, even wore hats to declare our MAGA allegiance. And why not? No other American President promised his voters that he would make America rich! Or Great? Or Safe? What did we have to lose?

On the day he was elected, I informed all my friends and relatives to buy, buy, buy...take advantage of what I predicted was a time in America like no other. We had a businessman with a PA Wharton School of Business education, a multi-billionaire who wrote the book entitled ***"The Art of the Deal"*** going to the White House!

And his economic advisors such as: Professor Art Laffer Ph.D. and Steve Moore, Visiting Fellow at the Heritage Foundation, Larry Kudlow, Director of the National Economic Council, who were considered by me as the best supply-side economists on the Planet! In addition, a great economic advisor named Peter Navarro, Director of Trade and Manufacturing Policy, Boston born and educated at Tufts and Harvard, Ph.D. is one of the best in the business world to negotiate our international trade deals.

As an MBA, to me, this was like a dream come true. And, as we eventually experienced from 2016, 7, 8 & 9, it was a hell of a ride while it lasted! Several trillion of dollars in riches given to the participants....he certainly did make Americans rich again...quickly, even for a short period of time!

The analogy that I will use here is one that I am remarkably familiar with and that is a company's business system, their processes, controls and the people, their organization and management.

Let us compare this business structure example to our current Federal Government system. To begin with, suppose we were a new CEO put in place by a Board of Directors. The company was seeking to not only survive in the 2016 - 2020 era, but to thrive, is quite a challenge.

As CEO, I would try to determine what the company's strengths and weaknesses were. In addition, I would evaluate and assess the current organization as the late Lee Iacocca did at Chrysler on a typical work-day. When he arrived as CEO Chrysler Corporation, he played a key role in its turnaround.

On the first day of his presence, he called each one of the 33 Vice-Presidents into his office, one by one, he asked the following question, and what do you do? I would have loved to be a fly on the wall that day. For later in the first day, after he asked this question 32 times, there was only one Vice-President left. So, let us relate this to our present POTUS situation.

On this first day, as Jackson once said, "To the Victor Belongs the Spoils!" Over 2000 opposition party appointees were deeply entrenched into the system. Trump's predecessor, on his first day, fired every single one of those G.W. Bush appointees. In addition, he threw out all his processors Executive Orders immediately.

Today, my best guesstimate is that there still are over 1900 opposition appointees still in the so-called swamp. In the 2016 National Election, the District of Columbia's voters, in round numbers, gave POTUS Trump's opponent 282,830 votes (91%), his supporters gave him 12,723 (4%).... do the math! Now you can see just how difficult a job the new USA CEO has.

Back to our analogy! Next, we would look at the organization's resources: who they are and how they are organized and what specific function is required considering the current worldwide situations. By situations, I mean our competitors, our standing in the marketplace. Using the Jack Welch School of Business practices when he was at GE, you are either first or second in the marketplace or you were gone!

Here in Florida, in wintertime, the annual exodus occurs. Retirees from the Northern USA and even our dear friends from Canada, flock South to escape the cold of Winter, the days of snow, ice, and darkness. These are the lucky ones, who survived all the dangerous events of the 20th and so far the 21st Centuries. And the snowbirds as we are called, are then followed by the Spring Breakers and Easter crowds until the warm season appears up North!

Again, the three levels of rich appear centered around communities that have the amenities to satisfy the many levels of self-actualization.

And we, in the first panic of the USA, are searching for the same of answers…when can we return to our real homes?

And more importantly, what has happened to our dream of 2016…of making America rich again! For we all thought we were on the right track finally after all these years of toil! All my retired friends and family and neighbors liked the Trump Wall Street Rally. And suddenly almost overnight, the three plus years of our 401K rewards were erased…gone!

We bought into the American dream again, as we did as new adults going to school, working at menial jobs, elevating ourselves up the corporate ladder and saving for a rainy day as much as we could!

Now the dream seems like a nightmare for all Americans. We cannot even enjoy the freedom of being free…a standard practice for over 250 years! I am now on Day 29 of the shutdown of USA!

Shutdown the USA and you are asking for trouble! In some states with little virus impact, people are kept from even worshiping on these for some are their holiest days Passover and Easter celebration weeks. Rigid rules of not going out is not going over well with these folk's virus or no virus!

USA Civil rights are being impacted! Even the Attorney General of the USA offers his concerns of the freedom and right to congregate, especially for religious services. Some religious leaders arrested for trying to hold church services!

Reporting to you today April 7, 2020, it appears that the stock market is on its second day of a rally. Why? I say to myself, is it going up? Future earnings certainly will not return to normal for a long time? And we cannot go to a Federal Reserve Quantitative Easing (QE) 3, 4, 5, 6? Or can we?

Look the Dow is at 22.890, up 233 points, Nasdaq 7938, up 27, S&P 2687, up 24! But trending down, perhaps it is those short sellers again making a market. Buy high, sell low and all the rest of us try to buy low and sell high?

Gold today trades at 1,677 down 19! I every time I look at it, recall my great Northeastern University Finance I Professor Dave Macy, DBA Harvard, and PHD EE MIT, telling us on the first night of my Northeastern University Class in Boston to write this down:

"Buy gold at $32 an ounce"!!!. "And one day you won't have to work again!"

We all looked around and thought, anyone here have $32 in their pockets…all were attending on the new GI Bill just signed by LBJ! Not me, I said to myself! I am housebroke, married with two kids with a brand-new home loan and new car loan too! I never even thought to take out an equity home loan for buying gold. Who did? Did you?

For 137 million hard working Americans are eligible to sign up for a 401K. However, only 50% of us sign up!

For those who did from the first opportunity in the early 1980s a nice nest egg has been accumulating. Yes, we have seen serious swings but oner the long haul, like compounded interest rates are able to retire like our parents never dreamed about!

Opportunity knocks every single day in America. The worse times for some can be the best times for others. Perhaps as my Dad said many times, those with the money later can buy those dream houses for pennies on the dollar and he saw it happened, again and again, during and since the last and only Depression in the USA.

I recall just years ago beach homes were selling for half of what they are now. Perhaps that dream home in Naples will go for a realistic price! We can all still dream cannot we? For we are those crazy Americans!

9. MAGANOMICS: C+I+G: Boom or Bust?

"The Dangers of Irrational Exuberance"! *Allen Greenspan, USA Chairman Council of Economic Advisors Speech 1996*

Photo 9.0: Times Square, NYC March 2020 Take cover! (NY Times Photo)

When I first taught Managerial Economics at the Graduate level in the early 1980s, I needed to also learn Reaganomics! There were no books published yet on the new supply-side economics. However, I persisted, having learned about the 1950s Keynesian to the Milton Friedman Era and now a new POTUS Reagan Era.

With a supply-side emphasis, we covered how different a Republican platform vs a Democrat one that drove the capitalist machine called the USA! FDR rescued us from a Depression by Fed Government Programs that got the people back to work. WWII helped greatly!

POTUS Trump's Economic Program, designed by Professor Laffer, et al, had the same emphasis. Workers pay taxes, non-workers, do not, it is that simple.

And in the USA, only 50% of our population pay Federal Income Taxes.

What if you cut corporate income taxes…where does the money go? Does it cause more expansion as the Trump strategy desires? What about the "worker bees" or "bottom feeders" as our off-springs, highly-educated generation calls us?

Besides the pain and suffering and humble reactions of unemployment and job loss and disrespect…what and where are our crumbs cry the masses?

In my humble opinion, someone or many needs to be fired for sleeping at the switch or not knowing where the switch was! So many Fed Agencies, could have even made up many reasons to avoid the stock market crash…how about for health reasons…most of the traders are now sick! No one (except some of our fake news media) would criticize that one for shutting it down!

How about there being no plans, rules, or road map for dealing with a pandemic? There are none! As Bill Gates said in 2015, there are no War Games being played on the Corona virus! But there will be soon after a high-level, Blue Ribbon Committee will be established to investigate the Panic of 2020!

Certainly, the Don, as we then New Yorkers at the time called him, can find someone who has some street smarts in his personal group of Wall Street friends! Nobody helped him except VP Pence who did cut the mustard in my opinion! Remember readers, I am a Trump supporter and registered Republican! How about getting a Babson MBA in the job like me, I sent you my resume to the White House almost 4 years ago!

Almost a $10,000,000,000,000 loss...$10 Trillion in a month hit is justification for taking off a few heads! Again, this is in my humble opinion! Raise hell fellow Americans! This crash could have been prevented....someone needs to pay for the Pandemic of 2020!

MAGA Agenda – On April 5, 2018, then Chief of the Office of Management and Budget, Mick Mulvaney addressed the media with the following paraphrased explanation of "Maganomics". He cited first the 4th Qtr. of 2017 GNP growth rate of 2.9%! And our first 3 Quarters of the TRUMP Administration growth of 3.1%! Recall if you will, the actions that took place during this three quarters time.

1. Tax Reform – a reduction of Corporate levels to 24%!
2. Deregulation Reform – For every new one two needed to be dismissed!
3. Trade Re-Negotiation – especially China, Mexico & Canada who all were cleaning our clock, unabated, for years or to be more exact decades!
4. Energy Independence for USA – new technology, new underground pipelines, new ports for export!

Early on before running Donald Trump had many of the best economic gurus on the planet visit him several times to plan how as POTUS, he could address the economic plight facing him! One of my favorite economics Professors was and is Dr. Arthur Laffer who goes way back to the Reagonomics days.

These actions resulted from his recommendations and Trump like Reagan did as Governor of California, adopted all of them! Read their new book, "Trumponomics" written by Artur Laffer and Steven Moore who also was an economic advisor. Larry Kudlow did a fine job in the book Forward!

America had turned the corner after years of decline. A return to a time described as impossible by the opposition forces. A magic wand was even cited with the impossible statement of job growth by our former leaders!

The Nation reacted and in three years, the stock market climbed higher and higher. All the economic indicators had shown positive trends. Unemployment dropped to never reported levels; poverty declined as opportunities for work suddenly appeared everywhere even in formerly depressed areas of the USA. From the coal fields of West Virginia and formerly coal fields of PA optimism flourished!

As time passed from 2017, 2018 and 2019, despite an all-out effort to remove the POTUS, yes remove him, the USA economy responded to a new record level in all major economic indicators.

Big and small businesses and ordinary Americans now saw hope in their future whether in their jobs, opportunities, or savings accounts! Quite simply, people were more better off than they were on the day before election in 2016 by the new Maganomics economy!

Recall from your basic ECON101 Course, it is all about this simple formula: $C + I + G = GNP$ and whether you or your neighbor is in a recession, depression, or Boom! We all seek the latter rather than either of the former! We are after all Americans!

Now, after this one of a kind panics of 2020, can the supply side economics of Maganomics be applied again? History will certainly reflect these times. For what we now are faced with are demand side of the equation measures that must be implemented. A good start with the injection of the CARES ACT, a $2.2T plus the Fed $4T…QE3 or is it 4? Perhaps it will go to 5 & 6 before it is over.

And what about all this talk of returning to the USA all those now Chinese industries ranging from electronics to medicines to furniture, auto parts and on and on? Where will we get the factory workers? Who of our off-spring wants to work in dismal factories for long hours at meager pays, certainly not mine with graduate level degrees from prestigious US colleges and Universities! How about yours?

Senator Lindsey Graham, GA is now sponsoring a bill to import 40,000 Chinese workers to back-fill the gaps caused by the CORIS-19 Virus. Is this the answer? I saw first-hand on my China visit, how hard-working people they were in the city of Shenzhen, with all the massive manufacturing factories there.

And what will happen to China if all these people are suddenly unemployed? Isn't that the reason we sent them there in the first placed, to prevent WWIII?

MAGA = C+I+G is the magic formula that needs to be re-applied again as in 2016!

How do we get consumers back to the workplace? The C (Consumers)! Can we create new workplaces now known as essential industries such as: pharmaceuticals, safety devices, medical devices, semiconductors, defense apparel, the basics: food, clothing, and shelter commodities we no longer can take for granted?

Now for the I (Investment): The Banks, homebuying loans, small business incentives, tax breaks, financial instruments such as bonds, perhaps tax free, new business creation, low interest loans with long payback periods.

And finally, G (Government): Made in America, America First expenditures to help grow the new USA Job creation program. Incentivize entrepreneurship, reduce Small Business taxes! Let us become the first and second sources of supply again before one world order became first!

And remember the multiplier and accelerator effects of money in circulation, the Federal Reserve holds the Trump cards here!

10. Past & Present World Panics!

"We have everything to fear, the threats are all around us!" COB "The $Panic of 2020!"

Visiting Italy in 1990, my tour guide was a nice, gentle Lady with a Ph. D. in History. She explained the wonders of the Roman Colosseum in vivid detail, who made it, when, and what occurred there. Outside, I was amazed when she showed the touring party, a large empty field where crowds of over 300,000 celebrated the chariot races on weekends! Sure, beats the NFL small crowds of nearly 100,000!

On our break, I asked her if she had ever been to the USA and what was her favorite city there? She replied, "yes, several times!" I liked San Francisco the best, she continued. Would you like to live in the USA, I replied? "No! No! Never!" she exclaimed! Why, I continued? "Too violent a place, I see it daily on CNN!"

Amazing what our modern communications networks can do, reporting 24/7/365 around the planet! Shaping even highly educated people's opinion and reinforcing their thoughts and perceptions of places, events, things, and ideas. Sometimes causing news forming addictions for a daily dose just to satisfy one's curiosity.

Today, in 2020, a world-wide panic is occurring, almost unheard of, after all little is taught in our education systems about the subject! Few are interested in it anyway, since it seems like happening long ago, far away, in the distant past.

The Year 2020AD will change that for everyone! Even 911 in 2001, seems like yesteryear for most of who live beyond the East Coast of the USA. Traveling frequently to the West Coast then, folks there did not feel the hit like we East Coasters, for it was 3,000 miles away and did not affect them. For those of us who were there, however, we can never forget that horrifying day. But all America will be touched by the panic of 2020!

Photo 10.0 NYC World Trade Center On 911! (NY Times Photo)

Our forefather's motivation to leave their beloved homelands and come to America were caused by many catastrophes. In my Grandfather's Joseph home country of Sicily, it took several events, occurring almost simultaneously. Events, such as: The Bank of Italy's failure, the 1918 flu that took millions of victims and lastly volcanic activity! That triple hat trick would cause me certainly, and drive me, to escape from that heavenly, pastoral tourist attraction of today!

Let us now review some past disasters starting with 1900 when we lost 12,000 from a hurricane in Galveston, TX! San Francisco on April 18,1906 an earthquake took 3,400 lives! Galveston was hit again in in 2008 and 2017 with hurricanes.

The year 1914 in Italy an epidemic occurred. In 1922, there was a famine in the USSR! And in 1908, Italy had a violent earthquake!

The year, 1918 brought an epidemic to our friends from the North, Canada, and the USA and around the world! Three waves of illnesses passed through each country hit! 50 million perished in those waves of Spring, Summer and Fall seasons. One third of the Earth's population perished! And the flu hit us again in 1951 and 1978 and every year since!

In 2020, the regular flu is estimated to kill from 29.000 to 59,000 Americans! Not counting the Corona virus that may take out another 60,000 as of today's estimates!

Of course, in 1941, there was Pearl Harbor attack by Japan on the USA! 2,235 military personnel were killed in that attack!

And, lastly, the first USA homeland attacks of 911 when 2,977 and 6.000 injured in cities of NYC, DC and Shanksville, PA!

And let us not forget our participation in 20th and 21st Century Wars, some that continue after almost 20 years!

	World	USA	PA	NY
WWI	16-30M	116,516		
WWII	56-85M	405,399	26,554	31,215
Korea	1.5-4-5M	54,246	2,030	1,766
Viet Nam	1,353,000	58,209 282,000 Allied 444,000 VC 627,000 Civilians	1,859	2,546
Desert Storms I & II		4,800 Coalition. 30,000 Iraqi		
Afghanistan	47,000 to 62.000	2,440 1,720 Contractors		
War on Terror	586,423			

Table 10.1 War Casualties from 1940s (Wikipedia.org)

As one can see, mankind is the biggest source of conflict as nation after emerging nation seeks to acquire a better life or just lust for power and domination of the mass populations.

As Italian Economist Pareto observed years ago a vital few seem to control the trivia many as he so accurately described so many years ago. In the past century only a handful of dictators caused so much destruction and lasting damage to our unique planet.

One can only imagine if these forces were applied to conquering our real Earth enemies such as food shortages, diseases, elimination of poverty, homelessness, addictions, crimes, pollution, and all other mankind afflictions, what a wonderful world it would be to live in?

11. POTUS Daily Briefings: <u>Washington, DC</u>

"The BUCK <u>stops</u> here!"

POTUS Harry Truman 1946

Photo 11.1 POTUS & Corona fighting staff members 2020 (NY Times Photo)

Every single day for the month of March 2020, and now April, the POTUS and his designated TEAM of Heads of US Medical Laboratories and our top health agencies meet to inform the population of the plan and results of their plan to kill, dodge or avoid the "hidden pandemic enemy.

For my book readers information and to avoid redundancy, I have consolidated events into the plan and actions discussed ad nauseum in these news conferences.

<u>*O'Boyle's 2020 Rule*</u>*: If it sounds crazy, perhaps, it is crazy!*

Calendar Day, March 18, 2020, Wednesday.

More POTUS daily TV conferences. Today's focus is on how much money to give hundreds of millions of Americans; estimates are for $1000/per taxpayer. Bernie Sanders, US Senator from Vermont, a Socialist Democrat, from Vermont says $2000 a month for every family until the crises is over. Not bad if you are a millionaire as Bernie is! Are any of these measures the economic, medical fixes or defensive systems failure gaps corrective actions. Does not look like it to me, as the stock market again today hits the circuit breakers at 7% falling to almost 10% a day when the market remains open.

Let us review so far back as weeks ago when Wall Street and you and I is were hitting records for the 125 or 135th time since the Trump rally to a DOW 30,000 level.

The NASDAQ fell from a 9000 level then to today's 6800 and the S&P at 2300 from a 3000-point high. Treasury Secretary Mnuchin insists day after day to keep the market open for liquidity! Remember, there are no written rules or controls or anything yet on how to deal with Pandemics…we never had any, because we never had one!

We are essentially flying blind, without even the Kollsman Instrument invented aviation altimeter of 1929! I know this, because I worked there in in 1979, as a Director on the 50th Anniversary of Lt. Jimmy Doolittle's September 24,1929 successful first blind flight from Mitchell Field in Long Island, NY.

These are the economic situations that are occurring in the markets third week of decline. It reminds me of the story about killing an elephant on a safari. Shot after shot, the animals staggers still fighting to stay alive and after many,

many shots find the animal stumbling but still clinging to the finale of life.

When in distress call in the Marines! Not quite yet, however, but the Navy Ships Comfort and Mercy were deployed to both the East Coast and West coast by now as he describes himself our Wartime POTUS!

Photo 11.2 USNS Comfort arriving in NYC 3/30/2020. (NY Times Photo)

A POTUS moral boosting televised trip to Norfolk, Virginia saw the launching of the USNS Comfort weeks before scheduled thanks to an all-out 24/7 effort of personnel there.

This POTUS action was in addition to the USNS Mercy landing at the port of Los Angeles to add additional medical capacity to deal with the future COVID-19 victim surges there.

Photo 11.3 USNS Mercy heading for LA 3/2020 (NY Times Photo)

The USA is pulling out all the stops on assisting both the East and West coast with Naval Hospital ships activated to deal with the panic of 2020! See Web-Site: http://www.mercy.navy.mil/

President Trump holds his daily briefing Wednesday on the coronavirus pandemic. (Jabin Botsford/The Washington Post)

Photo 11.4 New 6-foot Rule in White House Brady Room!

As shown even the Daily COVID-19 Daily Briefing Social Distancing Rules are implemented at the White House Press Room (Brady Room).

All military reserves with medical specialties have also been activated. Quarantine States on the table to be done next.

For dealing with the COVID-19, Medical members of the Presidential Committee started to utilize and show to the public computer projections of dealing with the new invisible enemy.

Dr. Anthony Fauci, MD (Director National Institute of Allergy and Infectious Diseases since 1984) and Dr. Deborah Birx, MD (retired US Army Colonel, 29 years) Corona Task Force Response Coordinator, were the spokespersons mostly addressing questions on the daily TV briefings. Dr. Birx referred to the IHME Model (funded by the Bill Gates Foundation) as the standard statistical data base for projecting future prognostications and impact on our planet!

For your information I have taken the liberty to include some of the vital contents of this powerful model here. We start at looking at the home page of the Web-site!

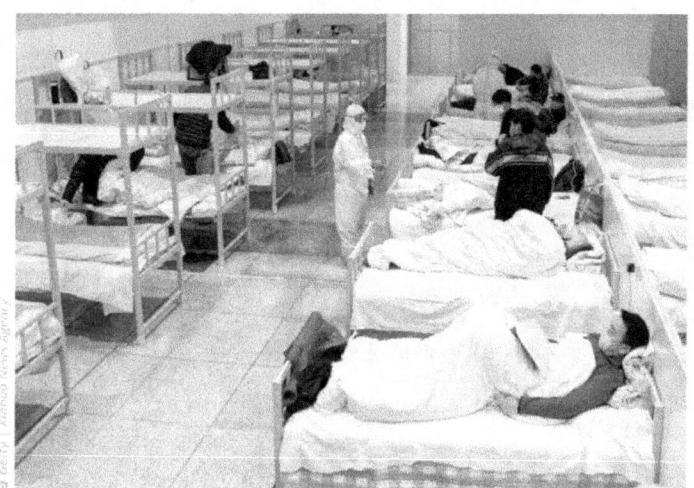

Photo 11.5 World Hospital Systems becoming overloaded! (NY Times Photo)

The preparation for the COVID-19 population peak forecast has caused a drive to build more units. Portable military hospital (MASH Units) ae suddenly appearing across the USA built by US Army Corps of Engineers.

Shocking to me as a former NASA Contractor is the absence of Fed Gov technology being used for daily tracking of COVID-19?

Daily Task Force updates appear to be using commercial models to manage the event?

The Gates Foundation in the State of Washington at Washington University is mentioned daily. So, let us look at it!

Photo 11.6 IHME Web-Site Home Screen

Note that a USA State by State tracking of all virus caused statistics are available. The model is very user-friendly and quite interactive. For the April baseline, I prepared Table 11.7 below to put the Panic of 2020 in proper perspective based on the results so far.

COVID -19 Scorecard on April 5, 2020 (Palm Sunday)

	World	USA	NYC
Contacted	1,260,104	331,234	4,758
Dead	69,082	9,458	159
%	5.48	2.86	3.3
Annualized	828,000	114,000	1908

Table 11.7 Daily Task Force Scoreboard on COVID-19

For a 30,000-foot level, it is hard I know for me to do this but remember our What if Scenarios. So, what if we compare stats in Table 11.7 USA and the World. For now, we seem to be handling the problem much better!

My annualized total with a look at the USA Annual Statistics available from another Fed Gov web-site: CDC.gov!

Data are for the U.S.A:

- Number of deaths: 2,813,503
- Death rate: 863.8 deaths per 100,000 population
- Life expectancy: 78.6 years
- Infant Mortality rate: 5.79 deaths per 1,000 live births

Number of deaths for leading causes of death:

1. Heart disease: 647,457
2. Cancer: 599,108
3. Accidents (unintentional injuries): 169,936
4. Chronic lower respiratory diseases: 160,201
5. Stroke (cerebrovascular diseases): 146,383
6. Alzheimer's disease: 121,404
7. Diabetes: 83,564
8. Influenza and Pneumonia: 55,672
9. Nephritis, nephrotic syndrome and nephrosis: 50,663
10. Intentional self-harm (suicide): 47,173

Plug-in the annualized COVID-19 model statistics from Table 11.6 above. You get 114,000, that number falls in just after our 6th cause of death, Alzheimer's Disease and our number 7, Diabetes!

However, upon additional analysis, adding COVID-19 to Influenza/Flu causes this to go up to Number 4 Cause on the CDC Top 10 List.

In NYC, as Table 11.6 shows, COVID-19 would rank after Cause Number 10, after Sepsis, that has 2,296 casualties annually.

We, the USA would then have, temporarily, a new number 7, COVID-19 to then deal with. Again, recall this is just a model an educated estimate. As Dr. Deborah Birx cautions we will have the accurate numbers at the end of this event!

Let us cover another computer model that is being used to track the CORVIS-19 Event! Johns Hopkins in Baltimore has an active web-site we shall now explore.

Table 11.8 Johns Hopkins Model results as of 4/7/2020

Country	Confirmed	Deaths	%	Recoveries
USA	368,241	10,986	3	19,828
Spain	130,675	13,341	10	40,437
Italy	132,547	16,523	12.5	22,837
Germany	103,375	1,810	1.8	36,081
France	98,984	8,926	9	17,429
China	82,697	3,335	4	77,393

(https://coronavirus.jhu.edu/map.html)

Several trends can be observed by Table 11.8 above. I added the % of mortality column. First, look at Germany an exceptionally low incidence of mortality! Secondly, the USA despite the highest number of confirmed victims maintains a low mortality rate. Thirdly, and one that is difficult to conclude is why recoveries seem to be all over the place with only China reporting a 94% survival rate! Perhaps all others are still early in their bell curve distributions and have not peaked (the apex) yet!

So, what would you do if faced with this dilemma…114,000 casualties from this new War, more than 911, Korea, Viet Nam combined? Or an economy closed-down and perhaps the same level and hundreds of $$Billions per month of shutdown. What are the trade-offs?

My answer is that we need a phased-in USA COVID-19 Recovery Plan like we did in Europe with the famous Marshal Plan. Our many USA Think Tanks (USA has 1,984 of them), Brookings Institute, Heritage Foundation, CATO Institute and Rand Corporation, all household names, can be given the charge to do this with minimum impact and maximum care in avoiding additional casualties.

My first selection from the IHME Model results is impact on Medical resources in the USA. One can see why POTUS took immediate action in helping the USA 'Hot Spots" like NYC, New Orleans and state of Washington and LA! Population density is a major factor in all these locations. And absence of any PPE for civilians also took a heavy toll. As seen in China, mask use even before the COVID-19 was standard practice there for years. This action perhaps saved many lives. Not until April did the USA recommend mask use now it is SOP!

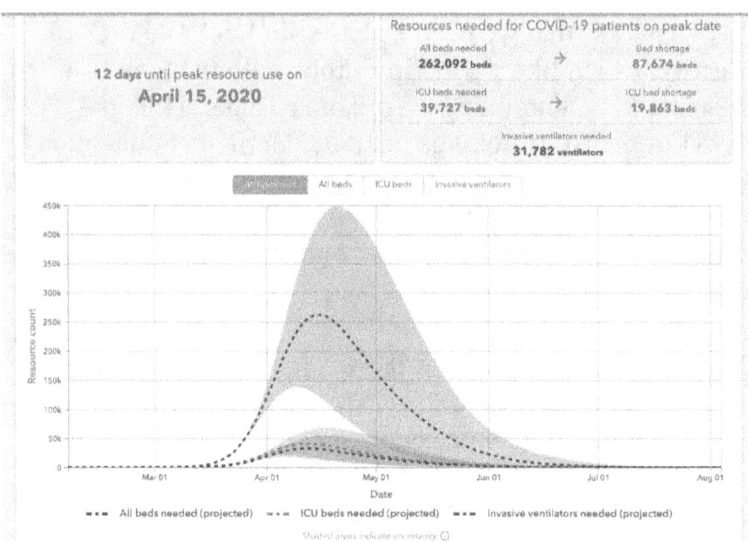

Exhibit 11.2 IHME Projected resources curve at peak date of 4/25/2020

According to the IHME Model, April 15, 2020, and as seen in Exhibit 11.2 a peak hospital bed period in three plots. First total projected beds, next ICU beds, finally the lowest curve, ventilators needed. Now you see for yourself where the daily numbers are coming form. Remember as Retired US Army Colonel, Dr. Deborah Birx says we will have a complete accurate model after this pandemic is over. This is a best estimate with 50% accuracy.

Here we are April 1. 2020 after the 15 Day Fed Gov Committee and POTUS recommendations. The Wall Street bleeding continues unabated. No circuit breakers daily trading just hovers at the edges of 7% down. Short sellers are still making $$ millions per day. Daily traders follow the insider's pack. I at times wish I too, had a Wall Street license to steal! One trader made $1.2 Billion in just one day speculating the UP/Down daily patterns. In the old days, a short seller needed an up market before continuing not today....short, short, short, all the way down!

Again the 2008 Wall Street measures are no match for this turmoil of algorithmic, microsecond 24/7/365 around the World trading.

Pre-programmed trading instructions for variables such as time, price and volumes....in microseconds! Something no human can even compete with or defeat!

The human toll has now reached 4,500 more than 911 just in NYC! Daily meetings now discuss the really bad news. USA Casualties may approach between 100,000 to 200,000 victims. Use of masks, a must do in China, now flips to a "may advise category".

Perhaps original positions were due to vast shortages from the medical community. We bought our weeks ago before the shortage. Along with boxes of throw-away gloves. Now it is feared that packages delivered to your home need to be guaranteed for a few days to kill the virus! What about the mail I ask?

Good news for the over 60s crowd today, 95% recovered, 193,000, a 5% casualty rate! HOT locations are the big city areas: NYC, LA even New Orleans calling the big numbers because of Marti Gras celebrations. Population density is the big concern as NYC Hospitals are reaching capacity. Temporary hospitals are being built to handle the peak periods that are forecasted yet to come perhaps in May or June!

New treatments are feverishly being explored. Several remedies have shown promise, but a vaccine is far off in the future. Old medical patient fixes such as replacing one's blood with a previous victim, who survived, also shows promise.

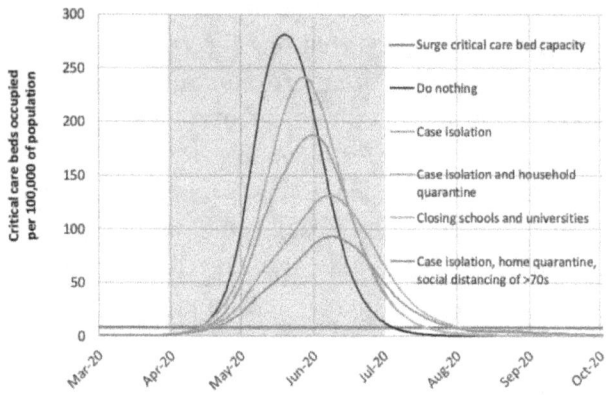

Figure 2: Mitigation strategy scenarios for GB showing critical care (ICU) bed requirements. The black line

Exhibit 11.3 Again, the IHME gives us a what if best/worst case result of dealing with COVID-19.

One can now see why the Easter date was a very risky one despite all our hopes this threat pandemic be over. As the state of conditions in China today in April of 2020 shows isolation, quarantine and social distancing are the best measures we can take for now without an immunization vaccine being available.

Dr. Jonas Salk, Pittsburg polio vaccine hero, where are you now is on all my generations mind today? For he saved our generation of the scourges of debilitating polio in the 1950s!

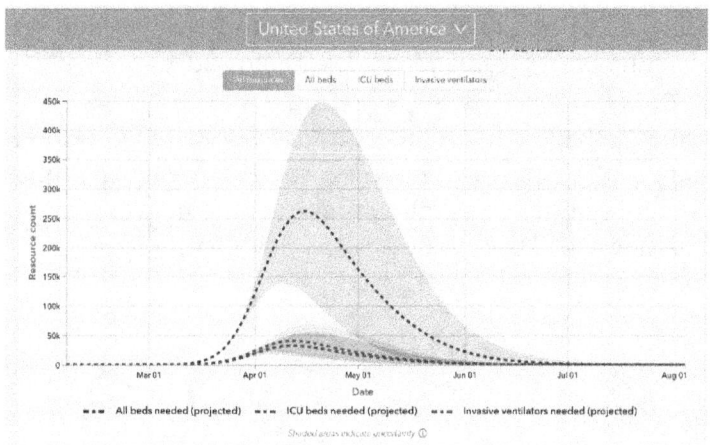

Exhibit 11.4 IHME Model USA Hospital Capacity needs for COVID-19

Daily meetings again and again re-enforce the need for washing one's hands for 20 seconds, frequently! Social distancing, wearing N-95 masks now, six feet apart separation and staying home avoiding human contact, the Medical Rx for the next 30 days!

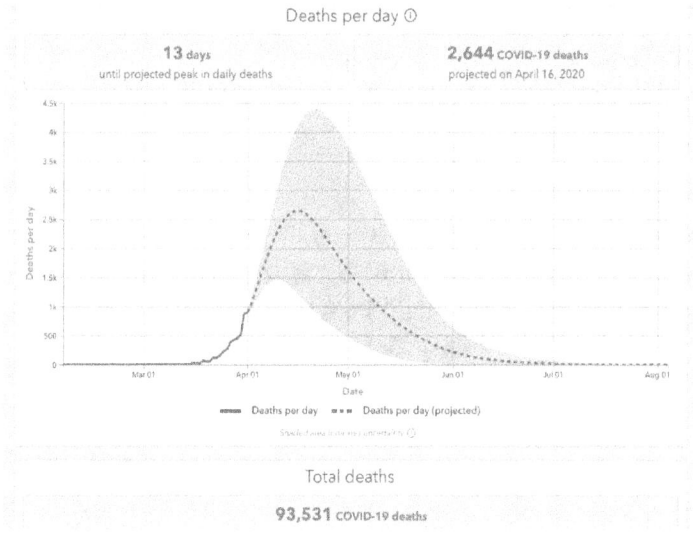

Exhibit 13.5 IHME model curves "where the rubber hits the road" Number of Deaths: Actual & Projected!

A dismal display is finally revealed by a solemn POTUS. Not since WWI or WWII have we, in the USA faced this level of mortalities he comments as opening his kimono on the bad news. 911 was not even one day's toll!

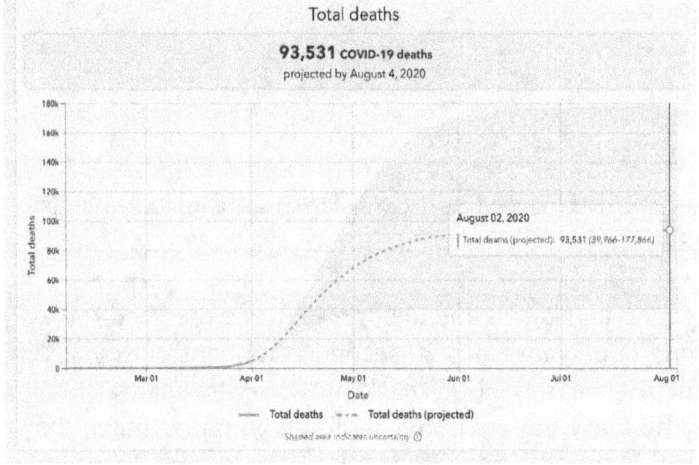

Exhibit 13.6 IHME Model best/worse-case plot of total deaths from COVID-19!

Projected total deaths approach the 100,000 level by August 4, 2020 as shown in Exhibit 13.6.

April 5, 2020, Palm Sunday, a highly religious day in the Western World is celebrated for all law-abiding God-fearing American citizens hunkered down on Day 20? Or is it 30, at home. Time seems to be a blur; no social discourse seems to be occurring except with efforts to unseat the incumbents!

Taking full advantage of my Apple TV, Amazon Prime and Netflix channels…never even knew I had so many options on my new high-definition TV! We are certainly spoiled society since millions still are on the other side of the digital divide and not even possessing a Wi-Fi connection! My family could not exist without one…including me!

Pandemic Day 28, April 9, 2020, Holy Thursday
Let us update our scorecard today. The computer models on the panic of 2020 are off by almost 30%. The figures that they predicted are now being significantly reduced. Totals that now fall in the 60,000 to 70,000 level for the United States of America. Still far exceeding 9/11 and Vietnam reported casualties.

The Wall Street's scene still hovers around the 7000-point drop on the DOW! Almost 1000 still down on the NASDAQ. But this week, it appeared to rise hundreds of points! A sign of optimism perhaps or a bottoming signal for all of us.

Body count as was used to report deaths in Vietnam battlefields approaches the 1000 person a day level just in the New York City area. Bed and ventilator predictions were also much higher than needed. Medical workers in the Hot Zones are being hit hard. The bell-shaped distribution curves have somewhat flattened in casualty count.

Yesterday, I hit a cabin fever peak. It is strange living near the Gulf of Mexico and not being able to take advantage of the wonderful winter lifestyle here. Took a trip to remote area beaches just for a breather but all the areas were blocked off. A few walkers on the local Causeway appeared, but the beach itself was empty.

Businesses that were booming a few weeks ago with the breakers are now empty. Someone bicycles with masks or exercising along route 19 N. on the great man-made bikeways stretching for miles down Pinellas County. Shutdown USA was in strict force. Gasoline here was down from the three-dollar program level II $1.80 at most beach stations some open.

For the first time people were working outside were wearing masks. Highway workers still on the job distancing from one another seem to have special masks like the ski jackets use the wear on the slopes of the snow-covered mountains. Complete protection continuously from the shoulders up to the eyes. A serious effort seems to have taken hold now across the sunshine state.

Approaching the May 1 time frame when we depart to go back to our mountains of Pennsylvania, we are concerned about the high rate of cases in major cities near New York, that seem to be known as hotspots also. Gov. Cuomo of New York appears on the national TV daily. He seems to be competing with Pres. Trump for all USA viewers? Some talking heads say that he could be the next Democrat POTUS after this is all over!

Blame and connecting the dots now seems to be taking place with the talking heads. China and United Nations organization WHO are the present targets. China for not letting the world know earlier of the upcoming pandemic. It was in 2015, when the Gates Foundation first warned the World. W.H.O the World Health Organization, who reported, it was not contagious and then reporting it late from the original start date of November 2019 Wuhan, China.

Again, perhaps the presidential blue-ribbon DC commission after the panic will provide us with answers or will fill in the blanks with a credible closing scenario. For some the truth may never be told even to our surviving generation.

Before finishing this book chapter on POTUS Daily Briefing, I too have a few questions of the medical staff, as I am sure you do too!

First Question! Since 2015, when the Gates Foundation spent $100,000,000 on the virus according to founder Bill Gates and alerted the World of this Corona Virus that could kill millions! Why was not an immunization developed then, by someone, since you are now saying that it is 12 to 18 months away?

Second Question! Who, when and for what reason, was the Wuhan, China Laboratory given $3.7 million dollars by the USA for studies on Bat virus research? Doesn't the USA have resources and existing Agencies to do that research? And what and where are the results of that Chinese Lab efforts?

12. Don't Just Stand There: Do Something!

"By today's attack on Pearl Harbor on December 6, 1941, the nation of Japan has unleashed a sleeping giant"
Admiral Yamamoto, Commander, Japan Imperial Forces!

Photo 12.0 Shooting of the POTUS Reagan and others outside Washington Hilton Hotel on **March** 30, 1981.

It was a day like many other fine weather days in Springtime, **March** 30, 1981 in DC, USA, that our new President Reagan, who just addressed a breakfast meeting and was rushing to return to his Oval Office. When outside the Hilton Hotel downtown, gun shots rang out, hitting several people in his heavily guarded security detail, including him and his Chief Press Spokesman James Brady, a Secret Service Agent and a local policeman were also hit.

POTUS was rushed to a local hospital and while still concious and asked if anyone in the operating room was a

Republican? Brady soon followed with severe head injuries that almost cost him his life. Both, after a long period of recovery, went on to do many great things. Jim Brady, however, was wheel chair bound almost the rest of his life!

Take note of the Photo 12.0 above, look at all the panic and chaos that ensued on that day. And to think of all that additional Secret Service protection measures and manpower instituted right after that historical event.

There are three kinds of people: Those who watch thing happen, those who make things happen and those who ask, what happened! I hope this writer is in the middle and certainly not the former or latter!

Several COVID-19 DC reactive measures were undertaken by our 535 political servants inside the Beltway, as we described it while workng there.

First out of the open corral, was another give away! It was referred to as the "Paycheck Protection Program" (PPP) love those DC bureaucratic buzz words, almost rolls off one's tongue….PPP! Even the kids can understand that one! The 4 million newly unemployed last month are signing up! As of this writing on Good Friday, April 10, 2020, we are rapidly climbing to almost the 1929 peak of 20,000,000 by almost 5,000,000!

Studying the '29 Crash reveals that year resulted in only a Recession, two consecutive USA Quarters of declining GNP! Even the Stock market went up again. However, over the long almost 10 year period of recovery even those who got out early sustained a declining life style, for America was changed forever.

Afterward, with fear of another Crash, investors and financial professionals instituted many systems corrective measures. However, years later in October 2008, almost 80 years later to be exact, we almost had another! And here we are approaching the 100 year mark and danger still lurkes us!

Inflated stock prices, Margin calls (10% down borrow the rest!) and slow reporting systems all led to the crash. Recall my chart on failures that takes several simultaneous circumstances to cause a failure…even with the best designs like the 737Max! In addition, the Smoot-Hawley Act passed on overseas tariffs to encourage sales, to no avail. All beginning to sound familiar? And in 1934, the creation of the Securities and Exchange Comission with future President Kennedy's father Joe in charge!

Quite an accomplishment for the new Irish citizens of the USA, who only a generation ago were faced with serious job descrimination when signs appeared saying "No Irish Need To Apply"! In fact, in New Orleans it was written that the Irish could not be listed as property assets or slaves, like the African Americans, since the Irish had no value! Watch the movie "***the Gangs of New York***" that filled in the USA history mural for me!

We called all those Fed Gov measures, "Corrective Action!" in the Space and hi-tech business. Our USA economy in March 2020, took a hit of $8 Trillion and counting… Anyone for $10T?

At NASA and in the high-technology business (read my books on "***My 50 Years in High-Technology*** " & "***Mission Success in Space***", we described several system critical functions that, when in place, acted as success factors to prevent product defects and failures from occurring.

When in rare times, a repeated systems anomaly or failure occurred, corrective action teams and measures were immediately initiated to mitigate the extent of these what could be termed as gaps in the process. The Web is filled with NASA Investigation Team Reports (nasa.gov) if you are interested. I participated in many of them!

These stock market sell-offs are ameliorated by such in place, almost automatic executions such: as a short sell, circuit breakers, oversight, and federal government controls. Many of them have been in place since the crash of '29 and were instituted by our beloved Pres. Kennedy's father Joe. As our first SEC Chairman Joe saw the pitfalls that existed in the 1920s stock trading process.

Among the corrective actions taken by the SEC Fed Gov Agency (4,694 Positions, Budget: $1.746 Billion!) were:

1. Transparency of Financial Instruments
2. Regulating Brokerages
3. Prohibit Insider Trading
4. Enforce Laws of Financial Industry
5. Cut back trading time
6. Circuit Breakers to prevent runaway
7. Risk Firewalls over Algorithms
8. Prevent Rogue Trading

Some from Item 6 to 8 are recent (2008) corrective actions to monitor computer trading (in microseconds now) and Rogue trading as what happened in France when a 31-year-old trader caused a $7 Billion dollar loss of a French Bank!

Since that time, a new computer software package by an organization named Progress, developed a new APAMA Risk Firewall that deals with Algorithm trading. It includes computer screen Dashboard database access and used development tools to monitor trading.

In our DC Agencies case, loss of focus, managing for results, and lack of accountability permeate the cast of thousands!

Chapter 13 next and Appendix One in this book will help identify what is needed, when, how and why!

13. Broken/Antiquated FED GOV Systems

…Housing crises

"We have met the enemy and he is <u>WE</u>!"
Overheard at a Sanders Associates PRIDE Program
Manager Review Meeting Circa 1970 Nashua, NH!

Photo 13.0 US DOD Pentagon recovering from 911 Attack!

Years ago, in 2008 to be exact, The USA panic at the time was over what DC called it "the Housing Crises"! Prior to 2008, the year that I finally retired for the third time at NASA, I looked around on my daily outside the beltway commute as a kid would do and watch the Cadillac Escalades, Jaguars, BMWs and Mercedes coming out of their secure, gated and walled communities off to their daily workplaces.

Wow! I said to myself how I would love to live there with the many upper-class Civil Servant and Fed Gov contractor families. This was a quite different place from the East Baltimore neighborhoods that I passed from my Baltimore

County living days. How could they afford these McMansions, taxes and upkeep, and new, luxury cars too, I wondered?

I was a Manager at the time and making a decent living. And as I said to one of my new hires who came from the Boston 128 area, "you won't become rich here, but you will live a decent life!"

What I did not know at the time, was that Fanny Mae and Freddy Mack were at the tipping point…overleveraged, the business community called it! The Housing crises of 2008 is what it became. Wall Street in just a few hours separated the pros from the newbies…as Generation X, refers to them.

It was a panic if you were living in one of those gated communities without a so-called CEO golden parachute package! The overblown bubble had finally burst. After 80 years of the Fed Gov private home ownership in the USA was in peril. Years later one of the best books of that era was one called ***"The Ascent of Money"*** by an Irish Ph.D. out of Harvard named Niall Ferguson! Later Niall did a great film (same title) that I bought along with his many great books.

In it, he begins with the Fed Gov policies on home loaning of the late 1930s and 1940 in Chicago. The maps at the time were redlined…on one side, you had poor folks, on the right the not so poor. The poor ones needed to pay extra interest rates to borrow money. The not so poor, got preference…a much lower rate. Quite like today, after the housing debacle of 2008!

Now, I am not talking about today rates, when even American Express charges more that 15% on your credit card and other companies can go up to 30%! Yes, look at your bill, the enclosed attachment with little letters and long legal words and percentages that we all just throw away every month...30%!

Our parents never used credit cards, no one trusted them, what if it was lost, they cautioned...cash was their preferred currency. As they often said, "In God We Trust, all others pay cash!"

Back then, only the mob got 20% in one's times of dire need. I remember the story I was told in Venice. When what appeared to be a closed Bank with Cross of David on it….an old-time lender only allowed to lend money in the boot of Europe! For it was a sin, at the time, to make interest money in Italy…against the law! I was told that only the Jew foreigners were given permission.

By reading "the Ascent of Money" you are going to fill in the missing dots on the housing crises of 2008! Hurrah to Professor Niall Ferguson for job <u>well done</u>…both the book and the movie!

Yes, another broken Fed Agency that was out of control and cost our first ever $Trillion in losses…$1.5T (again, add 12 zeros!). Jobless rate of 10% and the Fed provided $10T to federal Banks. Recall the name from 2008, Henry Minsky Harvard economist of 40 years ago. He observed that periods of stability and optimism---such as we had for the last 10 years, tend to amplify the dangers posed by the financial system based on easy money!**
  ** The New Yorker Sept. 17, 2008 "The Real Cost of the 2008 Financial Crises"

Based on what we covered so far, let us look at our nearly 250-year-old Federal Government in-place systems! Having worked in Washington nearly 20 years for the best federal agency in the government, NASA, I will use that as a looking glass and standard of comparison. At NASA, we had the best engineering talent on the planet! We had nearly 50 years of practice to come down the space science and art learning curve.

Our space systems were redundant in all designs. To protect Astronauts lives and to minimize failures. Our organizations had evolved to a fine-tuned structure of checks and balances from top to bottom. Our oversight also was redundant. Our designs had built-in proper Quality/Reliability/Risk requirements the same as Space/Aerospace industry controls.

We had the international standards. We had the highly skilled and trained personnel. We had excellent program managers and talented Teams. And we made a fly before buy standard practice.

What resulted was a high-level of mission success. Sure a few failures occurred, but it was an uncertain venture filled with undiscovered challenges! We were able to overcome many of the obstacles that were in our way. Now take these thoughts to our USA economic/financial/government sectors.

Specifically, let us focus first on our critical NYC Wall Street marketplace and what has happened over the past 40+ years to our present timeframe of 2020!

As a place where nearly 137 million Americans money is daily invested with dreams of a comfortable retirement as a goal deferring one's Federal taxes until a perhaps lower bracket is reached. And one's trust in their fiduciary's places where cold hard cash is placed at nearly the $25,000/year level (55 or older folks).

Today in 2020, this process has evolved to a fine skill and art in execution….the term often cited is " Algorithm Trading (AT)"!

Yes, AT has been slowly introduced to Wall Street for the past 40 years. I recall taking the first all computer MBA course program in the 1970s from Boston's famous financial institution and Babson College in Wellesley Massachusetts.

Our college was the first to have two large computer networks, one from Hewlett-Packard and the other from 128s innovated computer manufacturer called DEC or Digital Equipment Corporation (no longer are gone and absorbed by Hewlett-Packard toward the end of the 20th century).

During this timeframe, American business transitioned from a timesharing network with the Dartmouth Time Sharing System (DTSS), a popular business computer timesharing system and Lockheed (prior to Google) search engine sharing large populations of computer users. At the time, I was the first to have an ASR-33 teletypewriter internet connection in my office in the 1960s.

This technology was constantly evolving and eventually brought us Microsoft and Apple. Meanwhile, a Johns Hopkins computer geek named Bloomberg, yesterday's POTUS candidate Mike Bloomberg, the smart guy who spent almost $1 billion in a few weeks to unseat POTUS Trump. His Bloomberg terminals that today reach a population of 20,000 are leased for $25,000 a month according to public news reports and what does one get for that, a lot a hell of a lot of investment analysis power.

Together with today's powerful econometric models using daily worldwide news headlines, one insider can now unleash this power in microseconds creating trades at lightning speeds and almost anticipating world events and trends.

What you and I see, perhaps days later, is the human reaction to computer-driven events today's future trading around the planet from New York to San Francisco from Hong Kong to Shanghai to London, Paris, Zürich and all countries in between.

For example, look at the daily trading volume that occurred on August 24, 2018, almost a year from the beginning of our Trump rally boom peak. A triple volume day occurred, many investors took advantage of what was term a market "frothing" condition and returned to a cash position.

Now, let us play, a let us pretend game! Remember that game as kids? Add to it, a subset called the "what if" extension!

What if another epidemic occurs? What will happen to the US economy and the markets? Specifically, the Wall Street market. Sound far-fetched? Not really, this could be done, and computer modeling years ago could "crank it up" to a higher level of epidemic called a pandemic… Roll the dice!

Watch the Fortune 500 companies fall rapidly. No stopping it, there are no controls for pandemics to! Make money! Make lots of money! Remember folks, it is just like playing a video game!

Using what we called sensitivity analysis variables in every way shape and form can be done in this manner, after all computers are dumb machines that need smart programming!

In an age of supercomputers and network systems around the planet, world backups about, we have harnessed a power like never, a true autonomous, Artificial Intelligence or AI for short!

And who is controlling this new AI intelligence, the Feds, the SEC, the Secretary of the Treasury, The Federal Reserve system? We have no CIO! Has this been even addressed yet? Think about that, no government Chief Information Officer for the United States of America position! No Official Office either? Well, as we used to say, "what do you know?"

Our forefathers never dreamed about computers, let alone the power we possess in the USA in the 21st Century and our enemies are aware of this potential game changer.

If were able to land a man on the moon 50 years ago can you imagine what that technology can do after all these decades of evolution? We have cars that can drive and even park themselves! Hospitals that offer robotic surgery that we take for granted and trust wholeheartedly and their use.

But we have no COVID-19 immunization of method of treating it with lifesaving drugs either…a huge gap in our Medical practices!

If we and our offspring are to survive, we must stop thinking as they say, inside the box! Vertical thinking cannot be our only way! 20% of our brainpower will not do in 2020, we must unleash the greater 80% somehow, someway and computers seem to be the way out.

In 1980, I said to my Finance Class of students, that I read today in the Wall Street Journal, that in 10 years we would see more technology advances than the last 100 years What would they be I asked? The Boston Rt 128 high technology area class was filled with computer people from both industry and government, but no one had an answer.

Look around 40 years later… I'm typing this on two laptop computers (one called HP, the other Apple) using a Software Company called Microsoft's Office Suite and using my two iPads AI and iPhone Administrative Assistant to do my research and seeing time passing on my iWatch!

Nearby I have my wife chats on her Facetime iPhone to relatives around the other side of the planet. My iWatch alerts me to my new text messages. I search the World-Wide Web on my two iPads, one old, one very new. As I am writing this book, new companies replaced the old ones with new names like Facebook, Google, Amazon, Netflix and of course…Apple! And Apple's famous internet based iStore that no one even dreamed of years ago. Except a guy without a college degree, who had a grand vision, named Steve Jobs!

And the new young entrepreneur billionaires names like: Zuckerberg, Musk, Ellis, Bezos and even a new POTUS billionaire called Trump, not to forget Mr. Bloomberg, whose name is on the front page of every McGraw-Hill Business Week magazine that I subscribed to for almost 30 years.

Computer systems are built on what is called a platform. At the Fed Gov Agency, the Center for Disease Control (CDC) their platform is named Decipher!

The CDC presentation also directed the states to use a web platform called DECIPHER, which the agency was already using for food-related outbreaks, to report potential COVID-19 patients and confirmed cases.

But it wasn't until the week of Feb. 24 — the same week that the U.S. would discover its first case of community-acquired COVID-19 — that the CDC scheduled a training for states on how to use the platform, according to the documents. **Web-site -** https://www.arcgis.com/apps/opsdashboard/index.html#/bda7594740fd40299423467b48e9ecf6

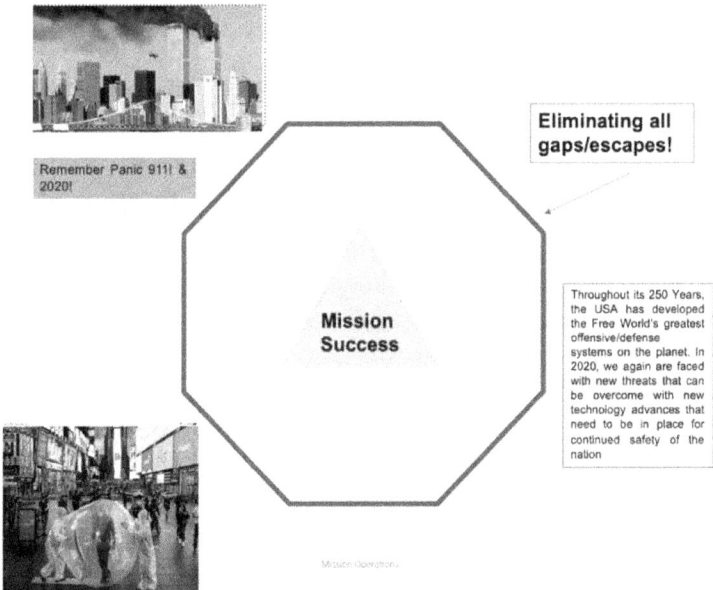

Exhibit 13.1 A desirable secured system is illustrated, impervious to outside or inside systems failure events enabling Mission Success.

As in almost every endeavor involving risk one can insure for circumstances unforeseen. However, uncertainty cannot be insured! Such is the reality of our man-made endeavors.

Exhibit 13.1 illustrates a secure, closed-loop BARRIER GAP FREE SYSTEM.

Perhaps as we used to say, even nuclear-hardened!

All 2020 Federal, State and local Agencies need to utilize Barrier Analysis to determine failure gaps in functions, organizations, goals (short/long term) objectives, redundancies and results. It is an amazing tool!

14. USA! USA!...Nobody Bats Zero!

"WE will only accept an Unconditional Surrender!"
USA 5-Star General Douglas McArthur 1945.

Photo 14.0: End of WWII Celebration Award Winning photo! (NY Times Photo)

On my first visit to China in 2005, I visited Johns Hopkins University Hospital as recommended by my gracious, B'more American Express Travel Agent. That visit's medical bill cost me over $600 to get special immunization shots! And I also received a preventative disease pitch on my upcoming trip.

I was given a detailed overview of precautions that were required prior to my trip. First, a highly qualified Nurse Practitioner told me " not to get a famous Asian Hong

Kong tattoo!" Blood poisoning was a common occurrence there with folks who visited cities on my travel itinerary.

Secondly, I would require a series of shots, a few in multiple doses over weeks. Thirdly, I was given a kit of medicine to take if sickness occurred. Be careful of the water you drink! No problem, I loved that German style beer (Captured German Factories from WWI) anyway was my reply! I wondered just how many travelers were taking these precautions...thank you, American Express Travel!

Our USA batting average over the last 100 years is remarkably high! Ted Williams, Boston Red Sox, had the last .400 season in MLB! USA won WWI & WWII and hit a speed bump in Korea and all other wars since. For my generation, we were all time winners over all our enemies!

For me, the WWII Victory ending that I can clearly recall was as a toddlers age, a weekend, Welcome Home Party given for my US Army Dad at a little apartment in Hillside, NJ.

His family of relocated coal crackers (17 brothers/Sisters) from Pennsylvania, celebrated for days! For the first time in my sheltered life, I needed to sleep on the floor. However, after crying to my Dad for a pillow, he threw one from the nearby couch and said, now get some sleep, which I somehow did!

I never knew that in his tour of duty he, along with his enlisted brothers, never thought they was going to return alive from overseas! They were familiar with fear, having survived the Plague of 1918 and Depression of the 1929-1939 Era.

Fighting and winning in WWII, gave them hope! Victory re-enforced it! Their winning momentum assured it! Dad lived until he was weeks from 90 and achieved more than even today's off-spring ever hope to attain!

We miss them in 2020, a lot! That **_Greatest Generation_** so well defined by Tom Brokoff in his best-selling book with that title.

We miss them so much that once a guy like Trump came on the scene with a WWII mindset…some of us, still alive heard slogans, MAGA resonating strongly among the American Electorate! Winning again, not just the hope and change slogans that did win over many heartlands' folks, but actions, not just words is what the heartlands of America wanted to see and hear!

Trump struck an inner patriotic American core value, we recognized from long, long time ago! A winning America!

This too shall pass some folks say. I say yes too, as the Keynesian saying goes "in the long run, we will all be dead!" No one has survived in 2000 years! Perhaps as he said, it was for all to focus on the short rather than long run. Knowledge folks today still debate the application of these words from long ago.

Americans love winners, and hate losing! It is in our DNA, lead, follow or get out of the way resonates with our Christian values. Making the impossible possible in every field, whether academia, technology, business, or society, we overcame all obstacles.

Americans can and will be overcome, whether climbing the Normandy Cliffs in WWII (thanks US Army Rangers) or taking down the Wall separating East/West Berlin as was done by POTUS Reagan! And, as so nicely put by my NASA Apollo hero, Director, Gene Krantz, **"Failure is not an Option!"**

Or as Adlai Stevenson II, US UN Ambassador voicing at the UN, showing U2 airplane photos of missiles in Cuba, that we will wait until hell freezes over for your answer of admission to the Russian Ambassador on October 25, 1962!

The American patriot words are so profound and elegant, I need to show you them here. Stevenson, a Princeton and Harvard Law schooled diplomat had his finest hour in American history!

"I want to say to you, Mr. Zorin, that I do not have your talent for obfuscation, for distortion, for confusing language, and for doubletalk. And I must confess to you that I am glad that I do not. But, if I understood what you said, you said that my position had changed, that today I was defensive because we did not have the evidence to prove our assertions, that your Government had installed long-range missiles in Cuba....

...Well, let me say something to you, Mr. Ambassador: we do have the evidence. We have it, and it is clear, and it is incontrovertible. And let me say something else: those weapons must be taken out of Cuba."

All right, sir, let me ask you one simple question: Do you, Ambassador Zorin, deny that the USSR has placed and is placing medium and intermediate range missiles and sites in Cuba? Yes or no. Don't wait for the translation, yes or no?

[Zorin] "This is not a court of law; I do not need to provide a yes or no answer..."

[Stevenson] You can answer yes or no. You have denied they exist. I want to know if I understood you correctly. ***I am prepared to wait for my answer until hell freezes over, if that's your decision.*** *And I am also prepared to present the evidence in this room."*

ADLAI STEVENSON'S UN SECURITY COUNCIL SPEECH (1962)

https://alphahistory.com/coldwar/adlai-stevensons-speech-un-security-council-1962/

Adlai Stevenson ran for POTUS twice, in 1952 and 1956 as a Democrat and lost to Dwight D. Eisenhower, Republican, 5-Star General and WWII Commander of all Allied forces in the European Theater of Operations, a hard to defeat competitor.

American history is filled with stories like these and my generation was raised to listen, read, study, know and understand them. From George Washington, to Abraham Lincoln, to Teddy Roosevelt, to Franklin D. Roosevelt, to Harry S. Truman, Dwight D. Eisenhower, John F. Kennedy, Ronald Reagan and now Donald J. Trump, the American glorious stories continues to motivate generations to follow the USA path, our amazing experiment of a special nation with freedom and justice for all!

And today in 2020, we again salute our first defenders, our emergency workers, our hospital staffs, Doctors, scientists, and our military, for they carry on our American traditions' day in, day out until this pandemic of 2020 is finally defeated.

God bless them all, and God help, and bless, our United States of America

15. ERISA: 1980s to 2020 (Your 401Ks!)

"The Biggest Scam of the 20th Century"! Op ed

Photo 15.0 Wall Street Trader on a bad day in 2008 (NY Times Photo)

As the above words declare, I have been a critic of the 401K since the stock market hit in the late 90s. I lost about $30K in one week, while I was deeply involved in writing a winning proposal for continuing my employment for another 5 years. I swore then no more losses for me…it was embarrassing to say the least for me with an MBA from Babson to lose even one dollar in the market!

And where are the significant few and we, the trivial many? Well, let us look back and learn again from our US history.

In 1974, a new Fed Gov Act was passed by our leaders in Washington, DC. The purpose of this act was to avert present generations from the inevitable, a bankrupt Social Security Program around since the 1930s. Recall earlier than that, the first officially passed Income Tax was passed at the federal government. This occurred in 1915. Can you imagine prior to the time our citizens were completely free of federal government oversight into our asset's incomes and fortunes! Yes, just over 100 years ago!

Fast forward to today 2020. Over 170 million of us are now enrolled in a 401K, 403B Federal Government Individual Retirement Programs. For example, I got hooked on mine in 1982, when I was sold on a "pay me now or pay me later" tax schedule.

Developed by the best political science, bureaucratic accountants, financial Wall Street wizards and best lawyers' money could buy at the time. In my several books, I referred to these as the biggest scams of the 20th century? Why, you may be asking? Good question alert reader!

Exhibit 15.2 US Stock Market Swings 2000 – 2009! (www.ambroker.com graphic)

21st Century Stock Market volatility is visually displayed in Exhibit 15.2. Take note of the five year up cycle followed by the sudden swift one-year downturn. Today this volatility continues daily with uncertainty abound in the chaos of Spring of 2020. We all await anxiously for the return to normalcy if that can ever be attained soon!

Here is the deal, as a worker bee, you can save some of your pay for retirement with a Fiduciary. These are firms like: Fidelity, Franklin Templeton, Edward Jones, Raymond James, or the Vanguards of the world. By placing a sum of money that goes untaxed until you retire the withdraw in later years, at a lower tax rate! Sounds good so far folks!

Yes, was my answer, everyone in the United States America loves to save on taxes, whether are they be local, state, county, city or Federal.

It is in our DNA as Americans going back to the Boston Tea Party and our rebellion of the 1770s. Tell me more you are saying. What could be wrong with this good Christian habit of saving?

All. As they say on Wall Street that was the upside. Now let us look on the downside!

First, you will be subject to the typical ups and downs based on our classic economic business cycle. On bull markets, all is well. You happily take the gains! You also compound the results. Love that Rule of 72! However, in bear markets you hate the losses.

Oh, you like know about the Rule of 72…the banks will never tell you. Neither will the Credit Card companies, or your DC Representatives who pass such measures.

I recall Bill Clinton signing the ATM Bill allowing fees to be charged for your bank cash withdrawals…up to $5 now, in some Banks.

And how about then Senator Joe Biden, 2020 POTUS hopeful, helping the big NY Banks, headquartered in Wilmington, DE, who charge now 30% for credit card use!

And neither are Republicans! But, remember the Republicans needed to vote it too. No preference here, equal opportunity!

The banks give you 2% on your savings if you are lucky. They charge you 30% on your credit card use, plus a fee to carry! Now, let us apply the Rule of 72.

$72/2 = 36$! Yes, you will double your money in 36 years…if you are alive! Now the banks! $72/30 = 2.4$ years…double their money in a little over 2 years! Got that from my Babson MBA!

For the past three years during Trumponomics or the MAGA years, we were feeling on a high never felt before. Financial investment ecstasy may be the words or "irrational exuberance" as we recall, said by the then Chairman of the Council of Economic Advisers, Alan Greenspan years ago. Up, up, and up over 130 times. How could you lose?

The American economy, in fact, the world economy was growing at unheard of levels. At Christmas times during the Trump era, shoppers shopped until they dropped. Even online companies like Amazon reached unheard of levels of sales. Yes, the USA was where the action was, and everyone wanted to share the wealth.

However, the talking heads on TV kept warning of a "heavy froth" occurring in the 2018/2019 calendar timeframe with dividends going to record highs.

My post-depression generation, in the back of our minds, recalled the frightening stories our fathers told us of that Depression Era. In their lives it was called the Great

Depression! And like this one is perhaps, an un-recoverable loss of one's fortunes may likely appear.

ERISA however may later help some recover even partial losses. In the Market fall of 2008, many clients executed protection in the original Fed Gov Bill.

Enforcement for ERISA in under the Department of Labor. Let us look at some important Act Consequences and Rules that may apply to all of us and them under this Fed Gov ACT!

As your Fiduciary, three specific responsibilities and consequences for your having your participation are:

1. Removal of their Fiduciaries duties.
2. Personal Liability for your losses.
3. Civil penalties like fines, even going to Jail!

These are serious matters and you as an American investor deserve enforcement. Now let us look at their duties they have signed up to legally!

1. Provide exclusive purpose…for you!
2. Protect investments
3. Monitor investments
4. Disclose investments
5. Execute IAW Plan, as documented
6. Avoid prohibited trades
7. Diversification of portfolio.

And as we noted earlier, the US Department of Labor (DOL) is responsible for enforcement. And the US Attorney General's Office will fully prosecute offenders of the law. Many involved were heavenly fined and served many years at our Club Fed resorts. This was done in so many cases during the Home Loan Crises of 2008.

Thank our country's Founders for this checks and balances form of government.

US DOL ERISA Web-Site:
https://www.dol.gov/general/topic/health-plans/erisa

16. Future Panics: N.B.C & Cyberspace!

"The only thing we have to FEAR is FEAR itself!" POTUS FDR Presidential Acceptance Speech March 3,1933!

Photo 16.0 Three Mile Island PA Nuclear Disaster March 28, 1979 (NY Times Photo)

N.B.C. is not the TV network we all grew up listening to over all these years. The letters stand for Nuclear, Biological and Chemical Warfare. Perhaps a forgotten threat from the 1950/60s. Up to Desert Storm, our military was trained in dealing with these horrifying weapons.

Just the other night, I watched a Jimmy Fox movie, great actor since 1990s when I spotted him on TV and predicted there is going to be a big star someday! The title was "Jarheads"!

I saw the PPE (personal protective equipment) of that period that protected from Gas, Chemical, Biological and

Nuclear attacks that could have been used in the battles at the time.

I cannot imagine covering one's self in that 100-degree heat of the desert environment. Got to give them credit for I doubt if few people could survive such harsh conditions.

Ok. You are looking for the answers of the future here, believe me if I knew them I would be making a "Back to the Future" logbook like the movie, that so nicely showed the new owner controlling every aspect of his world.

However, with my training and experience especially in graduate-level Creative Decision-Making courses, that I had the pleasure of teaching, I will take you through a few Scenarios and you decide if they are credible.

Scenario Number 1: A foreign-based advisory and declared enemy, plots to destroy America by launching a surprise attack on USA soil. Perhaps even using USA funding to pull it off as was done in 911! And using USA resources as weapons of destruction to launch, simultaneously, attacks that will seriously disrupt the opposing forces. And leave the USA in a state of disarray from which it can never recover.

Sound familiar…it soon will! Besides the USA will train the enemy forces, feed cloth and house them in a playground-like vacation luxurious resort location until their mission is accomplished. You are getting close reader….sound impossible? The result will be an attack that will yield more casualties than Pearl Harbor of 1941 on actual USA soil.

The answer to this scenario appeared on the very next day of the 911 attack, when 19 photos were shown on every newspaper in the USA…912 was the date! Do not say you were not surprised….hundreds of millions of us alive then were and still, to this day, are still wondering how it happened on 911…in 2001?

This is what happens to us when we become fat, dumb and happy for there are many less fortunate people on the planet who are envious of USA position as the leading country in the universe!

Scenario Number Two: Recessions 20XX?, 20XX?, 20XX?

A Middle East Country who admits publicly "Hates the USA!" plants a bio-virus seed in China to start a conflict between USA and China, that elevated could cause a World conflict again! And as on 911, a new weapon was deployed made with maximum damage to the entire free world.

See the 2017 movie titled ***"Unlocked".*** Perhaps the USA has on its prescription shelf, a drug that handles the virus would not this be a sad commentary after taking the economy down just a few days. Again, this can occur soon when similar situations that can occur, again and again.

Scenario Number Three: What we engineer is called worst-case scenarios: involving the basics food, water supply; paramilitary biological; pollution of all types.

Here, even the US Military MRIs are in short supply, Fed Gov priority have given to active duty personnel only. Water is also rationed as well as some essential foods. Power is not as plentiful, wide regional power grid outages are occurring in many southern states. The World Wide Web is up-and-down as it is our only form of personal communication.

What about projecting until June 2020? 80% of our restaurants have failed. Air travel is at an all-time low approaching pre-World War II levels. Big-name suppliers have laid off all maintenance personnel. Several serious air crashes have occurred. Fed Gov rules prohibit news of these events! Many private planes have taken their owners to far-off lands and properties for their own protection.

Scenario Numbers 5, 6, 7: Depression 20XX; Depression 20XX?; Depression 20XX?

Our last USA worldwide Depression occurred at the beginning of the 20th century 1918-1940. It began with the stock market crash of October 1929. And in one day the market completely collapsed.

Let us review the past recessions that occurred in the later part of the 20th century. There have been 47 Recessions in the USA since its founding as noted by the Bureau of Economics Research . Recall the 1953, '58, '60, '69, 73, '80, '82, '90, 2001, 2007, now 2020 Recessions! WOW! I remember them all! The complete USA Capitalist system of Business cycles in action! 12 Recessions since the 1950s, about one every 6 years average.

As indicated in scenarios two, three and four above previous recessions were limited to short-term negative impact on the US and world economies.

Scenario Number 8, 9, 10, we can now see how easy this task is once our brain is forced to think the unthinkable.

As of today, March 24, 2020, the Drudge Report listed 70 off-the-shelf medicines that may be a temporary/permanent fix for the coronavirus, called China virus sometimes by our POTUS or COVID – 19 as the latest media identifier.

It is difficult to connect the dots since one origin is Wuhan, China open marketplace cross animal/human virus. On the other hand, Bill Gates, formerly head of Microsoft talks about it in a video in 2015. And recently appeared on CNN to elaborate further on his Funds over $100,000,000 contribution to help eliminate it. .

And internet videos that say it was patented years ago! I checked it out! This was unfounded in that the Pirbright Institute was given two grants to combat corona virus, but the patent is for a chicken version not SARS-CoV-2. A vaccine is expected in 12-18 months. (USA Today, March 27, 2020)

In civilizations, techno-panics go back to earlier times such as the inventing of printing press in the Middle Ages, the invention of the lightbulb, when it was feared that the women and children would fall prey of intruders from the lighted home! Right up to today with anti-bacteria, super-bugs and germ warfare threats are shared all over the internet world population! Any advance today carries with it, new fears that spread like wild-fire!

With the now generations use of the World-wide web for their daily news fears that future reliability of information on-line, especially dis-information campaigns with popular web-sites are a new concern. These platforms are big target for the technophobes who perhaps see the dark side of all inventions.

17. Lessons Learned: After the Panics!

"America is great because she is good. If America ceases to be good, America will cease to be great!"
Alexis de Tocqueville (1805-1859) "*Democracy in America*"

Figure 17.1 NYC World Trade Center 911 Memorial (NY Times Photo)

Today on the site of the 911 tragedy, is a solemn memorial that identifies all the victim's names killed on that 21st Century Day of Infamy! Over 3,000 innocent civilians perished that day in NYC, Washington DC and over the skies of Pennsylvania. Almost 20 years later, we are still fighting in both locations of our then enemies, Iraq, and Afghanistan.

So, as they do at the military colleges after reviewing their many battles, what have we learned so far from our Panic of 2020 War! And if you are computer literate use of computers are permitted for this important exercise!

Well, we learned that human containment, local, regional, state, country isolation works to reduce pandemic casualties. We learned that testing plays a key role in dealing with accurate observing, reporting, and allocating resources to deal with such new unknown viruses even known ones such as COVID-19!

And after spending Trillions of US greenbacks on DC giveaways, perhaps we can re-focus all those Agencies to fill the many gaps existing in our defense and our many medical laboratory initiatives!

We also learned how intelligence, speed, proper, detailed plans, and preparation, even war/germ games, could have played huge parts in preventing a local epidemic from becoming a world-wide pandemic.

And we all learned a new acronym the hard way, PPE (Personal Protection Equipment): A N-95 mask, disposable gloves, hats, glasses, gowns, booties, coveralls all together save lives for our medical profession and even all people!

In 2015, Bill Gates, one the World's richest men, one of the founders of Microsoft. In his words, his Gates Foundation contributed over $100,000,000 to fight the Corona virus future epidemic, that he said at the time, was sure to come!

Too bad nobody was listening. Too bad nobody was listening! But if no one listens to a famous name like this what does J.Q. Public do? I repeated this twice, so it is clearly communicated! Just like TV advertising!

I certainly never heard of corona, only the kind that I consumed, after work, for relaxation, for years! See the Gates Foundation web-site (Gatesfoundation.org) for more details. Wish, I had one now in this, after 5 months of monotonous Florida heat…with a lime of course!

However, last year, I stopped consuming alcohol! They say that is the first sign of aging!

On March 24, 2020, the bleeding was stopped, temporarily! Today, as if by accident, one man on the planet, like him or hate him, put the tourniquet on the extremely sick dying, patient our USA and he or she is not a Republican or Democrat or socialist! He is the POTUS! Leader of the free World!

But why, you might be saying, simply because this the trade-off tipping point has been reached: the cost, the total cost of our USA shutdown and extended shutdown to a World-wide Depression, will clearly exceed the cost of dealing with the virus which today in the USA stands at a that fatality percentage of just over 3.4%.

So, XXX number of victims now or XXXXX more victims later…you do the math! This is what is at stake. At the White House garden town hall meeting 24th of March 2020 at 1 PM EST this subject was discussed in detail.

Here are today's Wall Street Stats and USA patient vitals of the USA marketplace are: 4/20/20

    Dow 23112…down 545 points

    NASDAQ 8,293…down 269 points

    S&P 2,745…down 81 points

Virus total round numbers: 4/20/20

   USA 810561 victims; Dead 43630, %: 5.4% Est!

   South Korea, the benchmark of the Planet: 2.2%.

And, 90% of the people who were tested and only 1.3 % had the virus. And of those who did 80% of them recovered. Again, all are rough estimates because we do not really know the COVID-19 infection rate or the case fatality rate?

As they used to say in the Space business, take your engineering hat off and place your Manager's hat on! Look at the following table for Wall Street Stock Market Crises.

Table 17.0 Comparison of S&P Declines during Crises!

Dates of S&P 500's largest declines	Black Monday (8/25/87-12/4/87)	Gulf War (7/16/90-10/11/90)	Asian Financial Crisis (7/17/98-8/31/98)	Tech Bubble (3/27/00-10/9/02)	Financial Crisis (10/9/07-3/9/09)	U.S. Credit Downgrade (3/10/11-10/3/11)	Trade War (10/3/18-12/24/18)
Downside shock	-33.5%	-19.9%	-19.3%	-49.0%	-56.8%	-19.0%	-19.6%
Next 12 months return	+21.4%	+29.1%	+37.9%	+33.7%	+68.6%	+32.0%	+37.1%

Source: Blackrock[5]

All American investors are standing by anxiously awaiting a return to normal timeframe when they hope to continue to be rewarded by the USA MAGA economy. Perhaps we can refer to earlier declines and forecast a time when conditions will recover from the present CORVIS-19 era of 2020.

Blackrock's Table 17.0 above shows worse case downside of two events at 56.8% and 33.5%. Both occurring with the Housing Crises of 2008 and Black Monday of 1987. All other five event periods averaged a 20% drop. Let us call it the downside risk!

Now to what we will call the upside potential! Only one, the housing Crises of 2008 shot up to almost 70%! Five had near 40% return in 12 months. One Black Monday only yielded 21.4% over the next 12 months!

Experts on the Street say this one is worse than the crises of 2008 already at a 20 to 30% drop and felling every week!

It all is riding on when the USA will be open again!

Epidemiologists say China's mammoth response had one glaring flaw: it started too late. In the initial weeks of the outbreak in December and January, Wuhan authorities were slow to report cases of the mysterious infection, which delayed measures to contain it, says Howard Markel, a public-health researcher at the University of Michigan in Ann Arbor. "The delay of China to act is probably responsible for this world event," says Markel.

"A model simulation by Lai Shengjie and Andrew Tatem, emerging-disease researchers at the University of Southampton, UK, shows that if China had implemented its control measures a week earlier, it could have prevented 67% of all cases there.

Implementing the measures 3 weeks earlier, from the beginning of January, would have cut the number of infections to 5% of the total."

On Trump's winning night, I watched the Dow Futures drop several hundreds of points in just a few minutes! Then like magic, it came back to normal! Wow! I thought, amazing! But nobody loved it like Mr. Trump.

"He has tweeted about the stock market at least 131 times since becoming president. He kept a running tally of stock market records — 135 by his last count, on Dec. 19. He personalized the rally, referring to "my stock market gains." *Stock Market's Gain Under Trump Vanishes* NY Times **By David Enrich and Matt Phillips** March 20, 2020

In 2015, just over five years ago, Microsoft's Bill Gates had an early warning about the panic of 2020. His unthinkable video on the subject covered intimate details of Americas unpreparedness for such a World-wide calamity.

In that video, Bill described the impact on the USA and identified immediate steps to mitigate or interdict the corona virus. Several actions mentioned in this book and unknown to me until I was deeply into writing it involved Federal Government investing meager funds and agency attention to this event. I am unaware of any action taken and from the circumstances; if any were it was inadequate to say the least!

However, no such Mission Control or Mission Operations exist for the new enemy of the pandemic 2020?

Perhaps using some of NASA's tools for **"Mission Success in Space"** (my New book) such as computerized scoreboards/dashboards and many of the controls described in my book on mission success can help in closing the present and future failure gaps that exist in both the W.H.O. organization and many government agencies almost helpless in the pandemic of 2020.

For if we only think that these events will happen every 100 years little corrective action will be done. But on the other hand, if we look at 2020 as a global warning for any new type of enemy, we will take the necessary precautions to interdict future debilitating events.

In fact, if it was not for the Boston-based College and University consortiums of computer model networks, we at the Federal level appears that we did not have any such capability! Even England's Imperial College had a model ready for analysis. No money in the over $6Trillion allotment allocated one cent for such capabilities. Another legal mindset solution to our panics.

Perhaps the Pandemic 2020 Blue-Ribbon Committee soon to deal with such USA disasters, will address this lack of USA Systems capability. Perhaps NASA can set one up or utilize existing Fed Gov resources to quickly implement one. For weeks, the POTUS was at the mercy of no system to cope with the pending disaster, no plan, no defense.

At least that is what appeared to exist during the daily press briefings. Even the Governor of NY seemed to use computer technology in his daily briefings!

We have such sophisticated systems as Air Traffic Control, Missile Defense Systems, Highway Traffic controls, Fire and so many other safety controls but no Pandemic Controls or even agencies…like the new Space Force!

Perhaps we need a Daily web-site after all it is the 21st Century, like the Daily weather Report so easily done with our fleet of Weather Satellites like GOES….thanks Goddard Space Flight Center! It would have our plans when the next attack comes: Weather, Biological or otherwise!

Or even alerts like our Big Bomb days like CONELRAD (Control of Electronic Radiation) Circa 1950s, thank you POTUS Harry S. Truman, 1951, or like Apple does today with their many Alerts on my iPhones!

Today, I looked at www.Worldometers.info to find out the latest story on COVID-19 world and USA statistics. Top level figures on April 18, 2020 remain at their peaks.

COVID-19	World	USA
Cases	2,263,032	710,272
Deaths	154,827	37,175
Recovered	581,161	63,510
Active	1,527064	609,587
Closed	735,988	100,685

Table 17.2 COVID-19 Status as of April 18. 2020

On Thursday, April 16, 2020 (Day 31) POTUS announced his guidelines for the **Opening Up of America Plan** an 18-page document that covers three phases of conditions of gradually opening stages that, once completed, restores a new normalcy to the USA. Specific instructions are given for individuals, employers, and specific types of employers.

POTUS Trump's Plan leaves the opening start date up to the individual 50 US State Governors if the new Plan's criteria are met satisfactorily.

See: https://www.whitehouse.gov/openingamerica/

As of today, Friday April 16, 2020 here are the latest Wall Street indicators:

Wall Street	Close	Status	2020 High
DOW	24,242	Up 704	29,569
NASDAQ	8,650	Up 116	9,838
S & P	2,874	Up 75	3,394
Transportation	8,234	Up 256	11.359

RUSSELL	1,229	Up 51	1,715
GOLD	1,694	Down 37	1,789
OIL	18.12	Down 1.75	66.60

Table 17.3 Wall Street snapshot of day after POTUS Opening of America Plan.

As one can see in Table 17.3, we have recovered leading indicators with amazing speed, despite our gloomy situation that exists in the USA today. The $2.2T + $4T Fed injection called the Corona Virus Aid & Economic Security Act (CARES ACT), Paycheck Protection Program (PPP) $350B, certainly helped bring it back from record lows.

However, volatility will continue once earnings are announced, dividends decline and so many bankruptcies occur. It took three years for the highs, can POTUS pull off a recovery in less time? Only time will tell, we surely will be watching!

We Americans deserve and want the best for our families now and in the future….call your Congress person and Senators…get it done America!

So, we are, where we are, Dear Reader… it is, what it is!

Is this the end of America as we know it? Or the beginning of the end? Or the end of the beginning? Take your pick America!

But for now, on this book, ***"The $Panic of 2020" Volume*** I, it is the end!

God willing, I hope to see you again when this is all over with my follow-on new book ***"The $Panic of 2020 Volume II"*** !

FINI!

Epilogue

Deep-down, I am an optimist, a WWII baby survivor, however, my training/education and 50 years of High-Tech management experience, working for large-scale Fortune 500 Enterprises, takes over in plights such as this ***"Panic of $2020!"*** nature.

I think of the honest, law-biding American patriots and their struggle to just survive, as I too was, exposed to in our lifetime. WWII, Korea, Viet Nam, Atomic Age, Desert Storms I & II, NASA's Challenger/Columbia and 911! How many panics can one endure in their lifetime and remain positive and financially whole?

As I remember from my darkest days in my life, always remember they can take away your job, take away your home, take away your family, take away your wife… Take away all your possessions! But they cannot take away your education, your training, your memories, your character, your faith, or your mind…your greatest gift and asset.

Live long and prosper, the best is yet to come. As we said in those dark days, we may lose our shirt, but we will keep our pants!

How about during our naive, blind-faith in our government systems youth that, in our lives, we wrote a blank check for! And, at the time, entering in our USA mandatory military service to protect, honor and preserve the USA…so help me God?

And as the Greatest Generation's off-spring, some of us whose Father's gave all in enemy battles and suffered their fate! Did not, what they did then, cause us to have a better life? And for our off-spring and even their children, whether it be resolving domestic or international events, did not they deserve better systems of government? Ready for any panic civilian or military challenge? Do they deserve this as their inheritance? Did their so-called leaders honor their oath of allegiance and office responsibilities as defined and sworn too? And walk the talk, with actions... not just sweet words?

Let us return to our USA Founding Fathers gifts written down for the ages...The Declaration of Independence, the Constitution, and the Bill of Rights! For we have drifted far from their founding intentions and future hopes, wishes and dreams for their newly formed America....land of the free and home of the brave! **God Help & Bless the United States of America!**

"Keep the faith, courage, enthusiasm" mantra from the movie "Company of Men"!

Bibliography

"China Road, Journey into the Future of a Rising Power" by Rob Gifford, Random House, 2007

"Where Have All the Leaders Gone" by Lee Iacocca Scriber, NY 2007

"No BS…Your MBA Primer!" by C.V. O'Boyle 2020

"Mission Success in Space!" by C. V. O'Boyle 2020

"My 50 Years in High-Technology" by C.V. O'Boyle 2020

"Democracy in America" Alexis de Tocqueville (1805-1859)

"Trumponomics" by Stephen Moore, Arthur Laffer, Ph. D. with Forward by Larry Kudlow St Martin's Press eBooks 2020

The New Yorker Sept. 17, 2008 *"The Real Cost of the 2008 Financial Crises*

Web-Sites Referral:

coronavirus.gov/

cdc.gov

healthdata.org

idigitalhealth.com/

afludiary.blogspot.com/

dol.gov/general/topic/health-plans/erisa

nature.com/articles/d41586-020-00741-x

whitehouse.gov/people/donald-j-trump/

yahoo.com/elections#donald-trump

alphahistory.com/coldwar/adlai-stevensons-speech-un-security-council-1962/

whitehouse.gov/openingamerica/

Appendix I: Future 2020 USA Security

First and foremost, we need to conduct a "Needs Assessment" for fixing the problem! There are many of them at on-line web-sites. Let us look at a few Models!

First, out of the University of North Carolina in Durham, a lovely campus with a great on-campus hotel that I was fortunately able to stay there one evening. And had a sumptuous several course dinners, with a sampling of the finest wines from around the World included! Focus writer focus!

Oh, yes the Needs Model! It is broken down into three major parts:

1. **Initiation**
2. **Data Collection & Analysis**
3. **Final Production**

As the NC Model is defined by the "What" that precedes the gap analysis (already shown in our book citing on Barrier Analysis) that is the how to close them. And followed by where the organization is and where they want to be! Nice KISS approach NC!

A few key questions are required!

> 1. *What do we need?*
>   Answer: 24/7/265 Security/Protection of USA & territories. Wall Street…new Rules for Panic times and Pandemic Events like 2020 or worse!

2. *When do we need it?:*
   Answer: Now! Spring 2020!

3. *How can the broken system be fixed?*

Answer: Use stop gap measures with existing resources. Meanwhile, lay out a Plan with a roadmap of how to get there on a short- and long-term basis!

Create War Room and Office of 2020 reporting directly to the POTUS to work to completion.

4. Who can fix it?
   Answer: POTUS & DOD (Representatives of all services) & NASA and it is Contractors! Add no one with vested interests!

5. *How long will it take?*
   Answer: 90 Days for Phase One of Three, not more than 6 Months for all Phases!

6. *What needs to be the results?*
   Answer: One Point of Contact (POC), One Responsible Agency reporting to the POTUS (Staff function), with backup protection, Plan B and Plan C…triple redundancy!

   Plus, two added POTUS Staff Offices: Assurance Management and Chief Information Officer (CIO)!

www.ingramcontent.com/pod-product-compliance
Lightning Source LLC
Chambersburg PA
CBHW050000230526
45465CB00003BB/1194